Second Treatise of Government

Second Treatise of Government

❧ JOHN LOCKE ❧

Second Treatise of Government

Edited, with an Introduction, by
C. B. Macpherson

Hackett Publishing Company, Inc.
Indianapolis • Cambridge

JOHN LOCKE: 1632–1704

Second Treatise of Government was
originally published in 1690

Introduction copyright © 1980 by the Estate of C. B. Macpherson
Printed in the United States of America

22 21 20 19 18   21 22 23 24 25

Cover design by Richard L. Listenberger
Interior design by James N. Rogers

For further information, please address
   Hackett Publishing Company, Inc.
   P.O. Box 44937
   Indianapolis, Indiana 46244-0937

   www.hackettpublishing.com

Library of Congress Cataloging-in-Publication Data

Locke, John, 1632–1704
     Second treatise of government
     Published in the author's Two treatises of government
under title: Essay concerning the true original extent
and end of civil government.
     Bibliography: p.
     1. Political science—Early works to 1700.
2. Liberty. 3. Toleration. I. Macpherson, Crawford
Brough. II. Title.
JC153.L85   1980   320'.01   80-15052
ISBN 0-915144-93-X
ISBN 0-915144-86-7 (pbk.)

ISBN-13: 978-0-915144-93-8 (cloth)
ISBN-13: 978-0-915144-86-0 (pbk.)

CONTENTS

Editor's Introduction   vii

Bibliography   xxiii

A Note on the Text   1

Title pages of the *Two Treatises*   2–3

1764 Editor's Note   4

Locke's Preface to the *Two Treatises*   5

THE SECOND TREATISE   7

Chapter I	7	
II	Of the State of Nature	8
III	Of the State of War	14
IV	Of Slavery	17
V	Of Property	18
VI	Of Paternal Power	30
VII	Of Political or Civil Society	42
VIII	Of the Beginning of Political Societies	52
IX	Of the Ends of Political Society and Government	65
X	Of the Forms of a Common-wealth	68
XI	Of the Extent of the Legislative Power	69
XII	Of the Legislative, Executive, and Federative Power of the Common-wealth	75
XIII	Of the Subordination of the Powers of the Common-wealth	77
XIV	Of Prerogative	83
XV	Of Paternal, Political, and Despotical Power, considered together	88
XVI	Of Conquest	91
XVII	Of Usurpation	100
XVIII	Of Tyranny	101
XIX	Of the Dissolution of Government	107

EDITOR'S INTRODUCTION

John Locke (1632–1704) wrote voluminously on subjects as diverse as the theory of knowledge, the reasonableness of Christianity, the case for religious toleration, the theory of money, and moral and political theory. In his own day and in the first half of the eighteenth century his fame rested mainly on his philosophical work: it was as the author of the *Essay Concerning Human Understanding* that he was so highly esteemed in England and Europe. Later in the eighteenth century his major work in political theory, the *Second Treatise of Government*, drew level with the *Essay* or even surpassed it in stature, especially in America where its doctrine of limited government and a right of revolution was widely referred to in the years leading up to the American revolution. Since then the *Second Treatise* has become a classic in the history of political theory. This seems odd at first sight. The *Treatise* was, as we shall see, professedly written only to justify a particular constitutional revolution in late seventeenth-century England; it was found useful again in justifying a particular colonial revolution in the late eighteenth century; but neither of those revolutions was in the next century so challenged as to seem in need of such an outdated defence. Locke's cause was decidedly the winner, both in England and America: the issues were settled. So why does his book now rate as a classic?

Part of the answer is that the Western liberal constitutional state, whose title-deeds Locke was one of the first to establish, is now under attack from new quarters—from the communist world and the third world, so that the liberal state is thrown back on the defensive and is glad to enlist in its support any plain hard-hitting case in its favour. Nothing could apparently be plainer than Locke's case, although on a closer look it turns out to be full of ambiguities. But the very ambiguities contribute to its stature as a classic, in two ways: they make the *Treatise* an excellent subject on which students may develop their critical abilities, and they make it an acceptable theoretical fall-back for publicists who accept the modern liberal state and society uncritically. What makes it especially valuable in both respects is that it is a case not only for the liberal state but also for liberal property institutions. Locke's case for the limited constitutional state is largely designed to support his argument for an individual natural right to unlimited private property. Defenders of the modern liberal state see, or sense, that that right is at the heart of their state. And nobody has made a more persuasive case for that right. On that, Locke is a much better bet than any of his contemporaries and most of his successors in the liberal tradition. The student of liberal theory is thus well advised to pay particular attention to the place of Locke's theory of property in his theory of government.

The *Second Treatise* is pretty well self-contained. Its companion piece, the *First Treatise*, is not essential to the understanding of the *Second*, though for Locke at the time it was important. It was directed against the principles of Sir Robert Filmer, whose books, asserting the divine authority of kings and denying any right of resistance, were thought by Locke and his fellow Whigs to be too influential among the gentry to be left unchallenged by those who held that resistance to an arbitrary monarch might be justified. Locke, having as he thought demolished Filmer in the *First Treatise*, simply summed that matter up in the first paragraph of the *Second* before going on to his positive case for limited government. Locke himself drew attention to the self-contained nature of the *Second Treatise* by inserting, apparently during the first printing of the *Two Treatises*, a new title for the *Second*: it had originally been simply "Book II" of the *Two Treatises*, and this subtitle was retained, but it was also given a separate title "An Essay Concerning the True Original, Extent, and End of Civil Government".

However, although the *Second Treatise* can stand by itself, in order to appreciate its whole meaning we need to know something about Locke's position in the intellectual currents of his time, and something about his role in the political and economic life of his country. We shall also have to look at other writings of his which reveal assumptions that he was taking for granted, especially the *Essay Concerning Human Understanding*, which contains a theory of human nature essential to the argument of the *Treatise* but not made explicit there.

Locke's Life and Times

Locke was born, in 1632, into a well-to-do family, of modest landed estate in Somerset. His father was a captain in the Parliamentary army in the civil wars of the 1640s. John was educated at one of the best schools (Westminster School, London) and then at one of the most famous Oxford colleges (Christ Church) where he lived, first as an undergraduate, then as a graduate fellow and teacher, from age 20 to age 34. At Oxford, where he concentrated on philosophy and medicine, he taught philosophy and took a medical degree. Afterwards, he kept up an active interest in medical science and moved in leading scientific as well as political circles, his scientific proclivities being recognized by his election to the prestigious Royal Society in 1668.

On leaving Oxford he formed a lasting personal and political connection with the first Earl of Shaftesbury, which brought him into the centre of the political life of the time. Beginning as Shaftesbury's personal physician he soon became his political confidant and researcher as well. Shaftesbury was leader of an influential group trying to compel Charles II to exclude his brother, the Catholic James, from the succession to the throne, and apparently prepared to resort to armed resistance if parliamentary means failed. They did fail; Shaftesbury was imprisoned for a time; but the plot went on, with Locke in the thick of it, attending conspiratorial meetings with and without Shaftesbury. There is strong reason to believe that while all this was going on, from 1679 to 1683, Locke's intellectual talents were brought into play to provide a theoretical justification for resistance to the sovereign; that he did write such a work; and that that work was the nearly complete draft of the *Two Treatises*, which only needed a few changes and additions to convert it in 1689 into a defence of the Whig Revolution.*

In 1683 Locke, for his own safety, fled to Holland, where he stayed until the Revolution made it safe to return to England, which he did in February 1689. From then until his death in 1704 he led a less hectic and, except for increasing ill-health, a more comfortable life, but still a very active one. Part of his activity was on the intellectual front: his published work in philosophy, and on Christianity and toleration, aroused much controversy and kept him busy publishing clarifications and defences of his position (though the *Two Treatises*, which he never acknowledged as his, did not).

He might well have rested on his renown as a philosopher, but his interest in affairs of state, and particularly in government economic policies, was so compelling as to induce him to serve, from 1696 to 1700, as one of the commissioners of the Board of Trade, the government body which advised on economic policy, in which he soon became the dominant figure. In this he was picking up again

---

*The case for this was convincingly made by Peter Laslett in 1956 and is presented in Part III of the Introduction to his authoritative edition of the *Two Treatises*.

the work he had done in 1673–75, before his exile, as secretary to an earlier similar body, the Council of Trade and Plantations. His interest in this is not surprising when one realizes that he was, already in the 1670s, a fairly wealthy man with substantial investments in such things as the raw silk trade, the Royal Africa Company (the slave trade), and the Bahama Adventurers.*

It is clear that when Locke wrote the *Two Treatises* he was no unworldly scholar but a man of property, greatly interested in safeguarding established property institutions, much concerned with policies to promote the increase of the nation's wealth, and deeply committed to the Whig position, both when it was a conspiracy against Charles II in 1679–83, and an open conspiracy against James II in 1688, and of course when it had triumphed with the installation of William and Mary in 1689. The *Treatises* are a product of that experience, of a mind shaped in Oxford and reshaped in conspiratorial and commercial London.

Locke on Human Nature

Every political theory which sets out to justify or advocate a particular system of government, or a limited or unlimited degree of obligation of the citizen to the state, must rest on an explicit or implicit theory of human nature. The theorist must show, or assume, that the human beings who will have to submit to and operate the desired system do need it and are capable of running it. In the seventeenth and eighteenth centuries this was often done by postulating a supposed natural condition of mankind, or "state of nature", from which men had historically or would necessarily move by some sort of agreement into political or civil society. Hobbes, for instance, had pictured men as so contentious that they could not survive without handing over their natural rights to an all-powerful and self-perpetuating sovereign state, and rational enough to see the need to do so. Hobbes set out his theory of human nature quite explicitly in the first eleven chapters of *Leviathan*, before he even used the logical device of a supposed natural condition of mankind.

Locke, by contrast, opened the argument of the *Second Treatise* by plunging right into a supposed state of nature, but he used it not to depict men's necessary behaviour or motivation, as Hobbes had done, but to assert men's natural rights. To get Locke's postulates

*Details of his wealth and investments are given in Maurice Cranston's definitive *John Locke, a Biography.*

about human needs and capacities one must turn to his *Essay Concerning Human Understanding*. There, in the course of an argument that there are no innate principles, either logical or moral, he asserts that there are innate inclinations of the appetite which are constant, namely, "a desire of happiness, and an aversion to misery".* These need to be checked by rewards and punishments:

> Principles of actions indeed there are, lodged in men's appetites, but these are so far from being innate moral principles, that if they were left to their full swing, they would carry men to the overturning of all morality. Moral laws are set as a curb and restraint to these exhorbitant desires, which they cannot be but by rewards and punishments that will over-balance the satisfaction any one shall propose to himself in the breach of the law.**

He ends by pointing out that his denial of innate moral laws is not a denial of any moral law:

> There is a great deal of difference between an innate law and a law of nature; between something imprinted on our minds in this very original, and something that we being ignorant of, may attain to the knowledge of, by the use and due application of our natural faculties. And I think they equally forsake the truth, who running into contrary extremes, either affirm an innate law or deny that there is a law knowable by the light of nature; *i.e.* without the help of positive revelation.***

Locke's rudimentary sketch of human motivation is remarkably like Hobbes's more precise theory. Appetites and aversions are the mainspring. Unless they are checked by a law armed with rewards and punishments they will override all moral behaviour. The similarity with Hobbes is even more striking in the importance Locke gave to men's desire for reputation, as in an entry in his journal in 1678:

> The principal spring from which the actions of men take their rise, the rule they conduct them by, and the end to

---

*Book I, Ch. 3, sect. 3. This is the chapter "No innate practical principles" which in some modern editions is numbered Book I, Ch. 2.

**Book I, Ch. 3, sect. 13.

***Book I, Ch. 3, sect. 13.

which they direct them, seems to be credit and reputation, and that which at any rate they avoid is in the greatest part shame and disgrace. This makes the Hurons and other people of Canada with such constancy endure inexpressible torments. This makes merchants in one country and soldiers in another. This puts men upon school divinity in one country and physics and mathematics in another. This cuts out the dresses for the women and makes the fashions for the men, and makes them endure the inconveniences of all. This makes men drunkards and sober, thieves and honest, and robbers themselves true to one another. Religions are upheld by this, and factions maintained; and the shame of being disesteemed by those with whom one hath lived, and to whom one would recommend one's self, is the great source and director of most of the actions of men. Where riches are in credit, knavery and injustice that produce them are not out of countenance, because, the state being got, esteem follows it, as in some countries the crown ennobles the blood. Where power, and not the good exercise of it, gives reputation, all the injustice, falsehood, violence and oppression that attains that goes for wisdom and ability. Where love of one's country is the thing in credit, there we shall see a race of brave Romans; and, when being a favourite at court was the only thing in fashion, one may observe the same race of Romans all turned flatterers and informers. He therefore that would govern the world well had need consider rather what fashions he makes than what laws, and to bring anything into use, he need only give it reputation.*

Locke's appetitive men, desirous above all of the esteem of others, have however, like Hobbes's men, enough natural reasoning ability to conclude that they need to agree on those principles of morality "that are absolutely necessary to hold society together, which," Locke adds, "commonly too are neglected betwixt distinct societies".** Appetites unchecked would destroy society; they can be checked by a general recognition that some minimum rules of

*Quoted in H.R. Fox Bourne: *The Life of John Locke*, 1876, Vol. I, pp. 403-4.

**Essay*, Book I, Ch. 3, sect. 10.

morality are needed. There is some ambiguity as to whether those rules need to be enacted into positive laws with enforceable punishments. We shall find the same ambiguity in the *Second Treatise* where *sometimes* Locke sees such rules, which he calls the law of nature, as being generally acknowledged and observed in "the state of nature", i.e. without any government to enforce them, but *sometimes* argues that a government with ultimate coercive power is necessary to enforce them. This ambiguity allows Locke to argue in the *Treatise*, both that there must and can be an agreement to establish an all-powerful civil society against which the individual retains no rights, and that no such power can arbitrarily be exercised by any government. Both arguments were required, as we shall see, by his concern for individual property rights.

From the "State of Nature" to Civil Government

Locke, like Hobbes, introduces the "natural" condition of mankind not as an historical condition existing before the emergence of civil society but as a logical abstraction from the essential nature of man. Though Locke does say later that it may also have been an historically prior condition (as in §§ 100–112 of the *Second Treatise*),* he presents it first as a logical deduction from the supposed nature of man and the supposed intentions of the Creator, which in turn are deduced from the observable biological needs of man.**

From the presumed intention of the Creator it followed that men were naturally equal, in the sense that no-one had more power or jurisdiction than another, and were naturally free "to order their actions, and dispose of their possessions and persons, as they think fit, within the bounds of the law of nature", which forbids anyone harming another or destroying himself, and requires each to try "when his own preservation comes not in competition" to preserve the rest of mankind (§§ 4–6). This law of nature would be generally observed, but there would be some transgressors; hence some power to restrain them would be needed; and since there was no government, that power must be left to every man individually (§ 7), but only as much power as is necessary "for reparation and

---

*Hereafter all references to the *Second Treatise* will be simply to the numbered sections, §§.

**cf. "Natural Rights in Hobbes and Locke" in my *Democratic Theory: Essays in Retrieval*, Oxford 1973, at p. 229.

restraint" (§ 8). Locke assumes that there are few offenders: he sums up this picture of the state of nature by calling it "a state of peace, good will, mutual assistance and preservation" where men live together according to reason, and contrasting it sharply with a "state of war" which is described as "a state of enmity, malice, violence and mutual destruction" (§ 19).

If he had kept to that picture of a peaceable state of nature there would still have been some case for setting up government, for there would be the inconvenience of every man having to be his own judge and policeman, but it would not need to be a very strong government. However, Locke did not keep to that picture. As early as § 21 he asserted that one great reason for men quitting the state of nature was that in it "every the least difference" is apt to end in the state of war; and later (in § 123), when he had to explain why men would ever leave such a free and equal condition as the state of nature, the reason he gave was that in it each was "constantly exposed to the invasion of others", his life and property "very unsafe, very insecure", and his existence "full of fears and continual dangers".

This ambiguity about the state of nature simply reflects Locke's fundamental ambiguity about human nature. In the first picture men generally are naturally reasonable enough to impose on themselves individually the moral rules needed to curb their contentious appetites. In the second picture they are not: the greater part are "no strict observers of equity and justice" (§ 123), and none can secure themselves individually. Locke needed both these inconsistent assumptions about human nature in order to make his case, which was that individuals must be understood to have agreed to give up their natural rights and powers to an all-powerful civil society, but that the civil society (themselves when so united) could not conceivably have delegated absolute or arbitrary power to any government, but must be understood to have retained the right to alter the frame of government whenever they (acting by a majority of themselves) so desired.

The assumption that men were too avaricious to secure themselves individually was needed to explain why men who were created free and equal would submit their natural rights to any authority. The assumption that, on the contrary, they naturally acknowledged a law of nature and would claim only the limited power needed to restrain occasional transgressors, not an absolute or arbitrary power over others, was needed to show that they could not hand over, and hence that no government could be given, absolute or arbitrary power.

Locke's argument proceeds along those lines. In order to protect their lives, liberties and estates, individuals must have agreed to hand over to society "all their natural power" (§ 136), or "all the power necessary to the ends for which they unite into society" (§ 99) as judged by the society (§ 97), even including jurisdiction over their possessions (§ 120), and to be bound by laws made under the authority of society. The acts of the society are the acts of the majority at any time (§ 96). The society thus created can then set up whatever frame of government it prefers, and may change it whenever it wishes. But it is inconceivable that the society should ever give absolute or arbitrary power to any government, for two reasons. First, since individuals by nature do not have arbitrary power over their own lives or over the lives and properties of others, they cannot give arbitrary power to society, and therefore the society does not have it to give to any government (§ 135). Secondly, to hand over absolute arbitrary power would be contrary to the very purpose for which the society was established, that is, the protection of the life, liberty and estate of each member: if they handed over their natural rights and powers to an absolute and arbitrary government they would have less protection than they had in the state of nature where each could at least take protective action for himself (§ 137).

We may notice that both these arguments require the postulate of the peaceable moral state of nature, as set out in §§ 4–8. The first argument requires it because on the opposite postulate (of § 123) individuals would not, on balance, necessarily worsen their condition by handing over arbitrary power. The second argument clearly depends entirely on the postulate of the moral state of nature where men's power is said to be limited to what they need to enforce the moral law of nature, which is explicitly not arbitrary power. And we may notice that even on that postulate Locke's second argument is fallacious, for even in his moral state of nature there are some who do not obey the moral law, that is, who *do* exercise arbitrary power, so there *is* arbitrary power that could be handed over.

We may wonder why Locke did not see this difficulty, nor the even greater one that his case required both the two opposite postulates about the nature of man or the state of nature. We shall not be in a position to suggest an answer until we have seen the further content Locke put into human nature and the state of nature in his famous chapter on property (§§ 25–51). That chapter is quite rightly famous: it is Locke's unique contribution to the seventeenth-century debate about "the true original, extent, and end of civil government"; it fixed property rights firmly in the centre of all subsequent liberal theory; and it is essential to an understanding of Locke's chain of argument from the state of nature to the limited and conditional nature of governments' powers.

Locke on Property

We cannot here go into all the intricacies of Locke's doctrine of property rights,* but we may try to sort out the main lines of his argument, to notice the additional assumptions he makes, and to assess the significance of his conclusions about property for his general theory of government.

His announced purpose is to explain how, although God had given the earth and its fruits to mankind in common, there could be a natural individual right to private property. The explanation is deceptively simple. God had given the earth to men for their subsistence: there was a natural right to life; and therefore each had a natural right to take to himself what was needed for sustaining his life. Moreover, every individual had a property in his own person and his own labour, and so could rightfully appropriate to himself from the common whatever he mixed his labour with. By this reasoning there must be certain limits to the amount of rightful individual appropriation. First, anyone may appropriate only as much as leaves enough and as good for others, since *everyone* has a right to his own preservation. Second, one may appropriate only as much as he can use before it spoils, for nothing was made by God for man to spoil or destroy. And third, of course, one could appropriate only what he had mixed his labour with. Within these limits, appropriation of the land itself as well as its fruits was justified. On these grounds there was evidently a natural right to this limited appropriation, a right which did not require any consent of others.

Had Locke stopped there he would have done nothing to justify the property institutions of his own, or any civilized society, all of which upheld private property rights far in excess of those limits. But he did not stop there. He made a further assumption, that while

---

*For a fuller examination, see my *Political Theory of Possessive Individualism*, Ch. V, sect. 2, pp. 197 ff.

men were still in the state of nature they had introduced the device of money. This rendered inoperative the spoilage limitation, for one could now convert any amount of perishable goods into money, which did not spoil.

The introduction of money also transcended the limitation about leaving enough and as good for others. The argument here was not quite as clear. In the first three editions of the *Treatise* Locke simply left it that the introduction of money would lead naturally to extensive commerce, which would make it profitable for individuals to appropriate more land than they could use the product of, so that all the land would be appropriated, leaving none for others, and that this was justified because all had consented to the use of money. In later editions he added a new argument (in § 37): land which is privately appropriated is ten times as productive as land left in common, so even when the land is all appropriated there is more produce for everybody. There is not enough and as good *land* left for others, but there is enough and as good (indeed more and better) *produce* for them. The original requirement had been that private appropriation should leave enough to meet everyone's equal right to subsistence, and that requirement was still satisfied after all the land had been taken up.

The third limit, that one could appropriate only as much as one had mixed one's labour with, was also transcended, or had a quite different meaning, after the introduction of money. For when there was no land left, those without any would have to sell their labour, for wages, to those who had land. When B, C, and D sell their labour to A, their labour becomes A's property; it is then *his* labour that is mixed with what was in common: ". . . the turfs my servant has cut . . . become my property . . . the labour that was mine, removing them out of that common state they were in, hath fixed my property in them" (§ 28). Thus there was no limit to the amount one could appropriate by mixing one's labour with what had been given to mankind in common.

Locke has thus in effect removed all the initial natural law limits on individual appropriation, and has established a natural right to unlimited amounts of private property. It is important to notice that Locke has all this happening in the state of nature, *before* men entered civil society (§ 50). It is to protect this natural unlimited right that men agree to establish civil society and government.

And we may notice the further assumptions that Locke has made. Men are naturally desirous of accumulating more property than

they need (§ 48), and this is morally unobjectionable as long as
nothing goes to waste (§ 46). The agreement to the use of money
(which was what made unlimited appropriation worthwhile) did
not create any new moral right: all it did was to remove the
technical obstacle that had made it not worthwhile, or not possible,
for anyone to appropriate such large and unequal amounts of property: the moral right to do so existed from the beginning. He has
also assumed that men are naturally rational and moral enough to
make and keep bargains even without any government to enforce
them (§ 14): without that assumption the extensive system of
markets, commerce, wage-labour, and accumulation, could not
have been attributed to the state of nature.

So we have Locke's ambiguity about the nature of man extended
into his treatment of property: man is naturally infinitely desirous;
he is rational enough to see that to give that desire full rein he needs
to adhere to bargains and contracts; but his exorbitant desire will
lead him to disregard his obligations unless there is a superior
authority to enforce them. This is what requires the institution of
government. And that institution is required only when property
has become very unequally distributed. In the earliest times, "the
equality of a simple poor way of living, confining their desires
within the narrow bounds of each man's small property, made few
controversies, and so no need of many laws to decide them, or
variety of officers to superintend the process, or look after the execution of justice, where there were but few trespasses, and few offenders" (§ 107). It is only in this second stage of the state of nature,
after the introduction of money and inequality, that the need for
government became pressing. Locke has read back into the state of
nature a class division, of whose existence in his own society he was
fully aware,* between those who had accumulated and those who
had not—between owners and wage-workers.

This creates a further problem. If there was the class-division
before the institution of civil society and government, and if the
purpose of instituting them was the protection of this unequal property, why would those without property agree to enter civil society
and thus give up their natural right of protecting themselves? They
would have good reason to do so if they were to become full
members of civil society, for then they would be the majority. But if
they were full members they might use their majority power to

---

*This is made explicit in his *Considerations on . . . Money*, cf. my *Possessive
Individualism*, pp. 216–17.

legislate a levelling of property. Locke did not see this as a problem for he never intended them to be full members. He took for granted that the right to vote in elections to the legislature was to be confined to the propertied class. Representation of cities and counties should be in proportion to the amount they contributed in taxes (§§ 157–8), and taxpayers were assumed to be those who had "estate" (§ 140).

But while the non-propertied were not to have any voice in making the laws they were to be fully bound by the laws: everyone is obliged, whether "his possession be of land, to him and his heirs for ever, or a lodging only for a week; or whether it be barely travelling freely on the highway" (§ 119). Both the exclusion of those without estate from the law-making process, and their subjection to the law, were required by the very purpose of civil government, the protection of life, liberty *and estate.*

Limited and Conditional Government

Enough has been said about Locke's theory of property to show how central it is to his theory of government and how consistent it is with his ambiguous theory of human nature and the state of nature. The state of nature, now, in the chapter on property, treated historically, is divided into two stages, before and after the introduction of money and inequality. One inherent trait of human nature, the boundless desire for possessions, which could not operate in the first stage, is given full scope in the second. Another inherent trait, the ability to follow the dictates of reason, changes its character. In the first stage it is the acceptance, easy then, of the natural law: "reason, which is that law, teaches all mankind, who will but consult it, that being all equal and independent, no one ought to harm another in his life, health, liberty, or possessions" (§ 6). In the second stage, where men are no longer equal, "reason" becomes not a moral law but an ability to calculate what course of action is required to safeguard unequal property; and this kind of reason is to be found only in those who have accumulated some property.*

It is from this second stage of the state of nature that Locke has men agreeing to enter civil society and establish government. So he can, logically enough, insist that the agreement must protect the propertied against the non-propertied as well as against each other

*On this differential rationality, see my *Possessive Individualism,* pp. 232–38.

and against a possibly arbitrary government. This requires a frame of government which shall be under the ultimate control of the propertied. And that is precisely what Locke stipulates.

His argument against *arbitrary* government has attracted most attention, and it is indeed important. Men, being so appetitive and contentious, have no choice but to hand over all their natural rights and powers, including their jurisdiction over their own properties, to a sovereign civil society (§ 120), but it would contradict the purpose for which they did so if they were to authorize an absolute or arbitrary government (§ 137). Hence Locke's insistence that the right of taxation must rest with the majority of the people, or with the majority of their elected representatives (which means, as we have seen, the majority of those elected by the property owners). Apart from this right of taxation, which only the majority of their representatives may exercise, no government can ever have any right to take any part of any man's property without his own consent (§ 138). Even *absolute* power, which must sometimes be granted (as to military commanders over their subordinates), is not *arbitrary* power: it gives the power of life and death but not a power over a soldier's property (§ 139).

Not only are the powers of any government thus *limited:* the whole power of any constituted legislature, and therefore of any other part of a government, is *revocable:* the legislative power (which must be supreme within any frame of government) "being only a fiduciary power to act for certain ends, there remains still in the people a supreme power to remove or alter the legislative, when they find the legislative act contrary to the trust reposed in them" (§ 149, cf. § 222). The authority of any government is conditional on its performing the functions for which it was entrusted with power.

Locke thus asserts a right of revolution. And he turns the tables on those who would deny that right by arguing that when a government has acted contrary to its trust by invading the lives, liberties or estates of the subjects, it is the government, not those subjects who resist it, who are guilty of rebellion: by denying the natural law limits on its power the government does "bring back again the state of war" (the literal meaning of the Latin verb *rebellare*), and may justly be resisted or expelled by force (§§ 226–7).

The Lasting Appeal of Locke's Doctrine

Several reasons for the strong appeal of Locke's doctrine, in his own time and since, are now evident. Composed initially to justify resistance to Charles II over the right of succession to the throne, it became when published a justification of the Whig Revolution of 1688-89 by which James II was dethroned and replaced by William and Mary, on terms which reduced the power of the crown and increased that of Parliament. It supported the resulting Whig state, which was controlled by the propertied class. A century later the doctrine, backed by all Locke's prestige, was neatly and quite properly turned against the British state by the American colonists. And ever since, although it has needed some supplementing and revising, it has been an invaluable ideological support for the liberal constitutional state and the market society on which the liberal state has been built.

As a liberal ideology it has almost everything that could be desired. It starts with free and equal individuals none of whom have any claim to jurisdiction over others: this is a characteristic and essential assumption of the proponents of a liberal as opposed to a feudal or patriarchal or absolutist state. It acknowledges that these individuals are self-interested and contentious enough to need a powerful state to keep them in order, but it avoids the Hobbesian conclusion that the state must have absolute and irrevocable power: it does this by attributing to men a moral capacity to discover and generally stay within a natural law which forbids harming others: this too is essential to the liberal case, and of course is flattering and agreeable. Moreover, Locke makes a unique and ingenious case for a natural right of unlimited private property, with which society and government are not entitled to interfere: no-one, before or since, has come near his skill in moving from a limited and equal to an unlimited and unequal property right by invoking rationality and consent.

The confluence of his main lines of argument about government and about property right provides an eminently useable ideological underpinning for the modern liberal capitalist state. The many ambiguities and logical fallacies in his arguments can easily be overlooked, so honest and enthusiastic was his attachment to the liberal cause. He may well be said to have written the title-deeds of the liberal bourgeois state. Those who wish to question that title, or to reinforce it, may well begin by narrowly examining the *Second Treatise*.

BIBLIOGRAPHY

A. Other Political Works by Locke

First Treatise of Government. The best edition is that in *Locke's Two Treatises of Government, a Critical Edition with an Introduction and Apparatus Criticus* by Peter Laslett (Cambridge: at the University Press, 1960, 1964). Laslett's introduction is invaluable in establishing the dates at which the *Treatises* were composed, their printing history, and their relation to their time.

First Letter on Toleration. There is a convenient paperback edition in the Library of Liberal Arts (New York, 1950).

Two Tracts on Government, edited with an introduction by Philip Abrams (Cambridge: at the University Press, 1967). The first publication of two pieces written by Locke in 1660–62, in which he appears to be more authoritarian than in the *Treatises.*

Essays on the Law of Nature, edited with an introduction by W. von Leyden (Oxford: at the Clarendon Press, 1954). The first publication of another early work of Locke's, written shortly after 1660.

Some Considerations of the Consequences of the Lowering of Interest and Raising the Value of Money (1691). Not available in any modern reprint. While this is a technical work in economics, it reveals uniquely some of Locke's social and political assumptions.

B. Biography

Maurice Cranston: *John Locke, a Biography,* London: Longmans Green, 1957.

C. Studies of Locke's Political Theory

Richard Cox: *Locke on War and Peace,* 1960, Oxford: at the Clarendon Press.

John Dunn: *The Political Thought of John Locke,* 1969, Cambridge: at the University Press.

J.W. Gough: *John Locke's Political Philosophy, Eight Studies,* 2nd edition 1956, Oxford: at the Clarendon Press.

C.B. Macpherson: *The Political Theory of Possessive Individualism, Hobbes to Locke,* 1962, Oxford: at the Clarendon Press.

Gordon J. Schochet (ed.): *Life, Liberty, and Property, Essays on Locke's Political Ideas,* 1971, Belmont, Cal.: Wadsworth.

Martin Seliger: *The Liberal Politics of John Locke,* 1969, New York: Praeger.

John W. Yolton (ed.): *John Locke, Problems and Perspectives, a Collection of New Essays,* 1969, Cambridge: at the University Press.

A NOTE ON THE TEXT

Each of the first three editions of the *Two Treatises*, of 1689-90, 1694, and 1698 (the only ones published in Locke's lifetime), was full of printer's errors. Locke made extensive corrections, and some significant additions, in a copy of the third edition. The first subsequent edition to take full account of these changes was the sixth, published in 1764. The present edition of the *Second Treatise*, along with the title pages, original editor's notes, and Preface to the *Two Treatises*, is reproduced from the 1764 edition.

Two errors found in the 1764 edition which were not in any of the first three editions have been corrected in the present edition: in the second sentence of § 48 the "not" has been restored before "be apt", and in the last sentence of § 87 "no such common people" has been changed to the original phrase "no such common appeal". In addition, a few simple typographical errors have been corrected.

TWO TREATISES OF GOVERNMENT

BY IOHN LOCKE

SALUS POPULI SUPREMA LEX ESTO

LONDON PRINTED MDCLXXXVIIII
REPRINTED, THE SIXTH TIME, BY A. MILLAR, H.
WOODFALL, I. WHISTON AND B. WHITE, I. RI-
VINGTON, L. DAVIS AND C. REYMERS, R. BALD-
WIN, HAWES CLARKE AND COLLINS; W. IOHN-
STON, W. OWEN, I. RICHARDSON, S. CROWDER,
T. LONGMAN, B. LAW, C. RIVINGTON, E.
DILLY, R. WITHY, C. AND R. WARE, S, BAKER,
T. PAYNE, A. SHUCKBURGH, I. HINXMAN
MDCCLXIIII

TWO TREATISES OF GOVERNMENT.
IN THE FORMER THE FALSE PRIN-
CIPLES AND FOUNDATION OF SIR
ROBERT FILMER AND HIS FOL-
LOWERS ARE DETECTED AND
OVERTHROWN.
THE LATTER IS AN ESSAY CON-
CERNING THE TRUE ORIGINAL
EXTENT AND END OF CIVIL
GOVERNMENT.

1764 EDITOR'S NOTE

The present Edition of this Book has not only been collated with the first three Editions, which were published during the Author's Life, but also has the Advantage of his last Corrections and Improvements, from a Copy delivered by him to Mr. Peter Coste, communicated to the Editor, and now lodged in Christ College, Cambridge.

PREFACE

Reader, thou hast here the beginning and end of a discourse concerning government; what fate has otherwise disposed of the papers that should have filled up the middle, and were more than all the rest, it is not worth while to tell thee. These, which remain, I hope are sufficient to establish the throne of our great restorer, our present King William; to make good his title, in the consent of the people, which being the only one of all lawful governments, he has more fully and clearly, than any prince in Christendom; and to justify to the world the people of England, whose love of their just and natural rights, with their resolution to preserve them, saved the nation when it was on the very brink of slavery and ruin. If these papers have that evidence, I flatter myself is to be found in them, there will be no great miss of those which are lost, and my reader may be satisfied without them: for I imagine, I shall have neither the time, nor inclination to repeat my pains, and fill up the wanting part of my answer, by tracing Sir Robert again, through all the windings and obscurities, which are to be met with in the several branches of his wonderful system. The king, and body of the nation, have since so throughly confuted his Hypothesis, that I suppose no body hereafter will have either the confidence to appear against our common safety, and be again an advocate for slavery; or the weakness to be deceived with contradictions dressed up in a popular stile, and well-turned periods: for if any one will be at the pains, himself, in those parts, which are here untouched, to strip Sir Robert's discourses of the flourish of doubtful expressions, and endeavour to reduce his words to direct, positive, intelligible propositions, and then compare them one with another, he will quickly be satisfied, there was never so much glib nonsense put together in well-sounding English. If he think it not worth while to examine his works all thro', let him make an experiment in that part, where he treats of usurpation; and let him try, whether he can, with all his skill, make Sir Robert intelligible, and consistent with himself, or common sense. I should not speak so plainly of a gentleman, long since past answering, had not the pulpit, of late years, publicly owned his doctrine, and made it the current divinity of the times. It is necessary those men, who taking on them to be teachers, have so dangerously misled others, should be openly shewed of what authority this their Patriarch is, whom they have so blindly fol-

lowed, that so they may either retract what upon so ill grounds they
have vented, and cannot be maintained; or else justify those principles which they preached up for gospel; though they had no better
an author than an English courtier: for I should not have writ
against Sir Robert, or taken the pains to shew his mistakes, incon-
sistencies, and want of (what he so much boasts of, and pretends
wholly to build on) scripture-proofs, were there not men amongst
us, who, by crying up his books, and espousing his doctrine, save
me from the reproach of writing against a dead adversary. They
have been so zealous in this point, that, if I have done him any
wrong, I cannot hope they should spare me. I wish, where they
have done the truth and the public wrong, they would be as ready
to redress it, and allow its just weight to this reflection, viz. that
there cannot be done a greater mischief to prince and people, than
the propagating wrong notions concerning government; that so at
last all times might not have reason to complain of the Drum Ec-
clesiastic. If any one, concerned really for truth, undertake the con-
futation of my Hypothesis, I promise him either to recant my
mistake, upon fair conviction; or to answer his difficulties. But he
must remember two things.

First, That cavilling here and there, at some expression, or little
incident of my discourse, is not an answer to my book.

Secondly, That I shall not take railing for arguments, nor think
either of these worth my notice, though I shall always look on
myself as bound to give satisfaction to any one, who shall appear to
be conscientiously scrupulous in the point, and shall shew any just
grounds for his scruples.

I have nothing more, but to advertise the reader, that Observations stands for Observations on Hobbs, Milton, &c. and that a
bare quotation of pages always means pages of his Patriarcha, Edition 1680.

OF CIVIL-GOVERNMENT

Book II

Chap. I.   §. 1. It having been shewn in the foregoing discourse,

1. That *Adam* had not, either by natural right of fatherhood, or by positive donation from God, any such authority over his children, or dominion over the world, as is pretended:

2. That if he had, his heirs, yet, had no right to it:

3. That if his heirs had, there being no law of nature nor positive law of God that determines which is the right heir in all cases that may arise, the right of succession, and consequently of bearing rule, could not have been certainly determined:

4. That if even that had been determined, yet the knowledge of which is the eldest line of *Adam's* posterity, being so long since utterly lost, that in the races of mankind and families of the world, there remains not to one above another, the least pretence to be the eldest house, and to have the right of inheritance:

All these premises having, as I think, been clearly made out, it is impossible that the rulers now on earth should make any benefit, or derive any the least shadow of authority from that, which is held to be the fountain of all power, *Adam's private dominion and paternal jurisdiction*; so that he that will not give just occasion to think that all government in the world is the product only of force and violence, and that men live together by no other rules but that of beasts, where the strongest carries it, and so lay a foundation for perpetual disorder and mischief, tumult, sedition and rebellion, (things that the followers of that hypothesis so loudly cry out against) must of necessity find out another rise of government, another original of political power, and another way of designing and knowing the persons that have it, than what Sir *Robert Filmer* hath taught us.

§. 2. To this purpose, I think it may not be amiss, to set down what I take to be political power; that the power of a *magistrate* over a subject may be distinguished from that of a *father* over his children, a *master* over his servant, a *husband* over his wife, and a *lord* over his slave. All which distinct powers happening sometimes together in the same man, if he be considered under these different relations, it may help us to distinguish these powers one from another, and shew the difference betwixt a ruler of a common-wealth, a father of a family, and a captain of a galley.

§. 3. *Political power*, then, I take to be a *right* of making laws
with penalties of death, and consequently all less penalties, for the
regulating and preserving of property, and of employing the force
of the community, in the execution of such laws, and in the defence
of the common-wealth from foreign injury; and all this only for the
public good.

CHAP. II.

Of the State of Nature.

§. 4. TO understand political power right, and derive it from its
original, we must consider, what state all men are naturally in, and
that is, a *state of perfect freedom* to order their actions, and dispose
of their possessions and persons, as they think fit, within the
bounds of the law of nature, without asking leave, or depending
upon the will of any other man.

A *state* also *of equality*, wherein all the power and jurisdiction is
reciprocal, no one having more than another; there being nothing
more evident, than that creatures of the same species and rank, pro-
miscuously born to all the same advantages of nature, and the use
of the same faculties, should also be equal one amongst another
without subordination or subjection, unless the lord and master of
them all should, by any manifest declaration of his will, set one
above another, and confer on him, by an evident and clear appointment, an undoubted right to dominion and sovereignty.

§. 5. This *equality* of men by nature, the judicious *Hooker* looks
upon as so evident in itself, and beyond all question, that he makes
it the foundation of that obligation to mutual love amongst men, on
which he builds the duties they owe one another, and from whence
he derives the great maxims *of justice* and *charity*. His words are,

*The like natural inducement hath brought men to know that it is
no less their duty, to love others than themselves; for seeing those
things which are equal, must needs all have one measure; if I cannot
but wish to receive good, even as much at every man's hands, as
any man can wish unto his own soul, how should I look to have any
part of my desire herein satisfied, unless myself be careful to satisfy
the like desire, which is undoubtedly in other men, being of one and
the same nature? To have any thing offered them repugnant to this
desire, must needs in all respects grieve them as much as me; so that*

If I do harm, I must look to suffer, there being no reason that others should shew greater measure of love to me, than they have by me shewed unto them: my desire therefore to be loved of my equals in nature, as much as possible may be, imposeth upon me a natural duty of bearing to them-ward fully the like affection; from which relation of equality between ourselves and them that are as ourselves, what several rules and canons natural reason hath drawn, for direction of life, no man is ignorant, Eccl. Pol. Lib. 1.

§. 6. But though this be a *state of liberty,* yet *it is not a state of licence:* though man in that state have an uncontroulable liberty to dispose of his person or possessions, yet he has not liberty to destroy himself, or so much as any creature in his possession, but where some nobler use than its bare preservation calls for it. The *state of nature* has a law of nature to govern it, which obliges every one: and reason, which is that law, teaches all mankind, who will but consult it, that being all *equal and independent,* no one ought to harm another in his life, health, liberty, or possessions: for men being all the workmanship of one omnipotent, and infinitely wise maker; all the servants of one sovereign master, sent into the world by his order, and about his business; they are his property, whose workmanship they are, made to last during his, not one another's pleasure: and being furnished with like faculties, sharing all in one community of nature, there cannot be supposed any such *subordination* among us, that may authorize us to destroy one another, as if we were made for one another's uses, as the inferior ranks of creatures are for our's. Every one, as he is *bound to preserve himself,* and not to quit his station wilfully, so by the like reason, when his own preservation comes not in competition, ought he, as much as he can, *to preserve the rest of mankind,* and may not, unless it be to do justice on an offender, take away, or impair the life, or what tends to the preservation of the life, the liberty, health, limb, or goods of another.

§. 7. And that all men may be restrained from invading others rights, and from doing hurt to one another, and the law of nature be observed, which willeth the peace and *preservation of all mankind,* the *execution* of the law of nature is, in that state, put into every man's hands, whereby every one has a right to punish the transgressors of that law to such a degree, as may hinder its violation: for the *law of nature* would, as all other laws that concern men in this world, be in vain, if there were no body that in the state of nature had a *power to execute* that law, and thereby preserve the innocent and restrain offenders. And if any one in the state of nature may punish another for any evil he has done, every one may do so: for in that *state of perfect equality*, where naturally there is no superiority or jurisdiction of one over another, what any may do in prosecution of that law, every one must needs have a right to do.

§. 8. And thus, in the state of nature, *one man comes by a power over another;* but yet no absolute or arbitrary power, to use a criminal, when he has got him in his hands, according to the passionate heats, or boundless extravagancy of his own will; but only to retribute to him, so far as calm reason and conscience dictate, what is proportionate to his transgression, which is so much as may serve for *reparation* and *restraint:* for these two are the only reasons, why one man may lawfully do harm to another, which is that we call *punishment.* In transgressing the law of nature, the offender declares himself to live by another rule than that of reason and common equity, which is that measure God has set to the actions of men, for their mutual security; and so he becomes dangerous to mankind, the tye, which is to secure them from injury and violence, being slighted and broken by him. Which being a trespass against the whole species, and the peace and safety of it, provided for by the law of nature, every man upon this score, by the right he hath to preserve mankind in general, may restrain, or where it is necessary, destroy things noxious to them, and so may bring such evil on any one, who hath transgressed that law, as may make him repent the doing of it, and thereby deter him, and by his example others, from doing the like mischief. And in the case, and upon this ground, *every man hath a right to punish the offender, and be executioner of the law of nature.*

§. 9. I doubt not but this will seem a very strange doctrine to some men: but before they condemn it, I desire them to resolve me, by what right any prince or state can put to death, or *punish an alien,* for any crime he commits in their country. It is certain their laws, by virtue of any sanction they receive from the promulgated will of the legislative, reach not a stranger: they speak not to him, nor, if they did, is he bound to hearken to them. The legislative authority, by which they are in force over the subjects of that common-wealth, hath no power over him. Those who have the supreme power of making laws in *England, France* or *Holland,* are to an *Indian,* but like the rest of the world, men without authority: and therefore, if by the law of nature every man hath not a power to punish offences against it, as he soberly judges the case to require, I see not how the magistrates of any community can *punish an alien* of another country; since, in reference to him, they can have no more power than what every man naturally may have over another.

§. 10. Besides the crime which consists in violating the law, and varying from the right rule of reason, whereby a man so far becomes degenerate, and declares himself to quit the principles of human nature, and to be a noxious creature, there is commonly *injury* done to some person or other, and some other man receives damage by his transgression: in which case he who hath received any damage, has, besides the right of punishment common to him with other men, a particular right to seek *reparation* from him that has done it: and any other person, who finds it just, may also join with him that is injured, and assist him in recovering from the offender so much as may make satisfaction for the harm he has suffered.

§. 11. From these *two distinct rights*, the one of *punishing* the crime *for restraint*, and preventing the like offence, which right of punishing is in every body; the other of taking *reparation*, which belongs only to the injured party, comes it to pass that the magistrate, who by being magistrate hath the common right of punishing put into his hands, can often, where the public good demands not the execution of the law, *remit* the punishment of criminal offences by his own authority, but yet cannot *remit* the satisfaction due to any private man for the damage he has received. That, he who has suffered the damage has a right to demand in his own name, and he alone can remit: the damnified person has this power of appropriating to himself the goods or service of the offender, *by right of self-preservation*, as every man has a power to punish the crime, to prevent its being committed again, *by the right he has of preserving all mankind*, and doing all reasonable things he can in order to that end: and thus it is, that every man, in the state of nature, has a power to kill a murderer, both *to deter others from* doing the like injury, which no reparation can compensate, by the example of the punishment that attends it from every body, and also to secure men from the attempts of a criminal, who having renounced reason, the common rule and measure God hath given to mankind, hath, by the unjust violence and slaughter he hath committed upon one, declared war against all mankind, and therefore may be destroyed as a *lion* or a *tyger*, one of those wild savage beasts, with whom men can have no society nor security: and upon this is grounded that great law of nature, *Whoso sheddeth man's blood, by man shall his blood be shed.* And *Cain* was so fully convinced, that every one had a right to destroy such a criminal, that after the murder of his brother, he cries out, *Every one that findeth me, shall slay me;* so plain was it writ in the hearts of all mankind.

§. 12. By the same reason may a man in the state of nature *punish the lesser breaches* of that law. It will perhaps be demanded, with death? I answer, each transgression may be *punished* to that *degree,* and with so much *severity,* as will suffice to make it an ill bargain to the offender, give him cause to repent, and terrify others from doing the like. Every offence, that can be committed in the state of nature, may in the state of nature be also punished equally, and as far forth as it may, in a common-wealth: for though it would be besides my present purpose, to enter here into the particulars of the law of nature, or its *measures of punishment;* yet, it is certain there is such a law, and that too, as intelligible and plain to a rational creature, and a studier of that law, as the positive laws of common-wealths; nay, possibly plainer; as much as reason is easier to be understood, than the fancies and intricate contrivances of men, following contrary and hidden interests put into words; for so truly are a great part of the *municipal laws* of countries, which are only so far right, as they are founded on the law of nature, by which they are to be regulated and interpreted.

§. 13. To this strange doctrine, *viz.* That *in the state of nature every one has the executive power* of the law of nature, I doubt not but it will be objected, that it is unreasonable for men to be judges in their own cases, that self-love will make men partial to themselves and their friends: and on the other side, that ill nature, passion and revenge will carry them too far in punishing others; and hence nothing but confusion and disorder will follow, and that therefore God hath certainly appointed government to restrain the partiality and violence of men. I easily grant, that *civil government* is the proper remedy for the inconveniencies of the state of nature, which must certainly be great, where men may be judges in their own case, since it is easy to be imagined, that he who was so unjust as to do his brother an injury, will scarce be so just as to condemn himself for it: but I shall desire those who make this objection, to remember, that *absolute monarchs* are but men; and if government is to be the remedy of those evils, which necessarily follow from men's being judges in their own cases, and the state of nature is therefore not to be endured, I desire to know what kind of government that is, and

how much better it is than the state of nature, where one man, commanding a multitude, has the liberty to be judge in his own case,
and may do to all his subjects whatever he pleases, without the least
liberty to any one to question or controul those who execute his
pleasure? and in whatsoever he doth, whether led by reason,
mistake or passion, must be submitted to? much better it is in the
state of nature, wherein men are not bound to submit to the unjust
will of another: and if he that judges, judges amiss in his own, or
any other case, he is answerable for it to the rest of mankind.

§. 14. It is often asked as a mighty objection, *where are*, or ever
were there any *men in such a state of nature?* To which it may suffice as an answer at present, that since all princes and rulers of *independent* governments all through the world, are in a state of
nature, it is plain the world never was, nor ever will be, without
numbers of men in that state. I have named all governors of *independent communities*, whether they are, or are not, in league
with others: for it is not every compact that puts an end to the state
of nature between men, but only this one of agreeing together
mutually to enter into one community, and make one body politic;
other promises, and compacts, men may make one with another,
and yet still be in the state of nature. The promises and bargains for
truck, &c. between the two men in the desert island, mentioned by
Garcilasso de la Vega, in his history of *Peru;* or between a *Swiss* and
an *Indian*, in the woods of *America*, are binding to them, though
they are perfectly in a state of nature, in reference to one another:
for truth and keeping of faith belongs to men, as men, and not as
members of society.

§. 15. To those that say, there were never any men in the state of
nature, I will not only oppose the authority of the judicious
Hooker, Eccl. Pol. lib. i. *sect.* 10. where he says, *The laws which
have been hitherto mentioned,* i. e. the laws of nature, *do bind men
absolutely, even as they are men, although they have never any settled fellowship, never any solemn agreement amongst themselves
what to do, or not to do: but forasmuch as we are not by ourselves
sufficient to furnish ourselves with competent store of things, need-
ful for such a life as our nature doth desire, a life fit for the dignity
of man; therefore to supply those defects and imperfections which
are in us, as living single and solely by ourselves, we are naturally
induced to seek communion and fellowship with others: this was
the cause of men's uniting themselves at first in politic societies.* But
I moreover affirm, that all men are naturally in that state, and re-

main so, till by their own consents they make themselves members of some politic society; and I doubt not in the sequel of this discourse, to make it very clear.

CHAP. III.

Of the State of War.

§. 16. THE *state of war* is a state of *enmity* and *destruction*: and therefore declaring by word or action, not a passionate and hasty, but a sedate settled design upon another man's life, *puts him in a state of war* with him against whom he has declared such an intention, and so has exposed his life to the other's power to be taken away by him, or any one that joins with him in his defence, and espouses his quarrel; it being reasonable and just, I should have a right to destroy that which threatens me with destruction: for, *by the fundamental law of nature, man being to be preserved* as much as possible, when all cannot be preserved, the safety of the innocent is to be preferred: and one may destroy a man who makes war upon him, or has discovered an enmity to his being, for the same reason that he may kill a *wolf* or a *lion*; because such men are not under the ties of the commonlaw of reason, have no other rule, but that of force and violence, and so may be treated as beasts of prey, those dangerous and noxious creatures, that will be sure to destroy him whenever he falls into their power.

§. 17. And hence it is, that he who attempts to get another man into his absolute power, does thereby *put himself into a state of war* with him; it being to be understood as a declaration of a design upon his life: for I have reason to conclude, that he who would get me into his power without my consent, would use me as he pleased when he had got me there, and destroy me too when he had a fancy to it; for no body can desire to *have me in his absolute power,* unless it be to compel me by force to that which is against the right of my freedom, *i. e.* make me a slave. To be free from such force is the only security of my preservation; and reason bids me look on him, as an enemy to my preservation, who would take away that *freedom* which is the fence to it; so that he who makes an *attempt to enslave* me, thereby puts himself into a state of war with me. He that, in the state of nature, *would take away the freedom* that belongs to any one in that state, must necessarily be supposed to have a design to take away every thing else, that *freedom* being the foundation of all the rest; as he that, in the state of society, would take away the *freedom* belonging to those of that society or common-wealth, must be supposed to design to take away from them every thing else, and so be looked on as *in a state of war*.

§. 18. This makes it lawful for a man to *kill a thief*, who has not in the least hurt him, nor declared any design upon his life, any far-ther than, by the use of force, so to get him in his power, as to take away his money, or what he pleases, from him; because using force, where he has no right, to get me into his power, let his pretence be what it will, I have no reason to suppose, that he, who would *take away my liberty*, would not, when he had me in his power, take away every thing else. And therefore it is lawful for me to treat him as one who has *put himself into a state of war* with me, *i. e.* kill him if I can; for to that hazard does he justly expose himself, whoever introduces a state of war, and is aggressor in it.

§. 19. And here we have the plain *difference between the state of nature and the state of war*, which however some men have con-founded, are as far distant, as a state of peace, good will, mutual assistance and preservation, and a state of enmity, malice, violence and mutual destruction, are one from another. Men living together according to reason, without a common superior on earth, with authority to judge between them, is *properly the state of nature*. But force, or a declared design of force, upon the person of another, where there is no common superior on earth to appeal to for relief, *is the state of war:* and it is the want of such an appeal gives a man the right of war even against an *aggressor*, tho' he be in society and a fellow subject. Thus a *thief*, whom I cannot harm, but by appeal to the law, for having stolen all that I am worth, I may kill, when he sets on me to rob me but of my horse or coat; because the law, which was made for my preservation, where it cannot interpose to secure my life from present force, which, if lost, is capable of no reparation, permits me my own defence, and the right of war, a liberty to kill the aggressor, because the aggressor allows not time to appeal to our common judge, nor the decision of the law, for remedy in a case where the mischief may be irreparable. Want of a common judge with authority, puts all men in a state of nature: force without right, upon a man's person, makes a state of war, both where there is, and is not, a common judge.

§. 20. But when the actual force is over, the *state of war ceases* between those that are in society, and are equally on both sides sub-jected to the fair determination of the law; because then there lies open the remedy of appeal for the past injury, and to prevent future

harm: but where no such appeal is, as in the state of nature, for
want of positive laws, and judges with authority to appeal to, the
state of war once begun, continues, with a right to the innocent
party to destroy the other whenever he can, until the aggressor of-
fers peace, and desires reconciliation on such terms as may repair
any wrongs he has already done, and secure the innocent for the
future; nay, where an appeal to the law, and constituted judges, lies
open, but the remedy is denied by a manifest perverting of justice,
and a barefaced wresting of the laws to protect or indemnify the
violence or injuries of some men, or party of men, *there* it is hard to
imagine any thing but *a state of war:* for where-ever violence is
used, and injury done, though by hands appointed to administer
justice, it is still violence and injury, however coloured with the
name, pretences, or forms of law, the end whereof being to protect
and redress the innocent, by an unbiassed application of it, to all
who are under it; where-ever that is not *bona fide* done, *war is
made* upon the sufferers, who having no appeal on earth to right
them, they are left to the only remedy in such cases, an appeal to
heaven.

§. 21. To avoid this *state of war* (wherein there is no appeal but
to heaven, and wherein every the least difference is apt to end,
where there is no authority to decide between the contenders) is one
great reason of men's putting themselves into society, and quitting
the state of nature: for where there is an authority, a power on
earth, from which relief can be had by *appeal*, there the continuance of the *state of war* is excluded, and the controversy is de-
cided by that power. Had there been any such court, any superior
jurisdiction on earth, to determine the right between *Jephtha* and
the *Ammonites*, they had never come to a *state of war:* but we see
he was forced to appeal to heaven. *The Lord the Judge* (says he) *be
judge this day between the children of* Israel *and the children of*
Ammon, *Judg.* xi. 27. and then prosecuting, and relying on his *appeal*, he leads out his army to battle: and therefore in such controversies, where the question is put, *who shall be judge?* It cannot
be meant, who shall decide the controversy; every one knows what
Jephtha here tells us, that *the Lord the Judge* shall judge. Where
there is no judge on earth, the appeal lies to God in heaven. That
question then cannot mean, who shall judge, whether another hath
put himself in a *state of war* with me, and whether I may, as *Jephtha*
did, *appeal to heaven* in it? of that I myself can only be judge in my
own conscience, as I will answer it, at the great day, to the supreme
judge of all men.

CHAP. IV.
Of S L A V E R Y.

§. 22. THE *natural liberty* of man is to be free from any superior power on earth, and not to be under the will or legislative authority of man, but to have only the law of nature for his rule. The *liberty of man*, in society, is to be under no other legislative power, but that established, by consent, in the common-wealth; nor under the dominion of any will, or restraint of any law, but what that legislative shall enact, according to the trust put in it. Freedom then is not what Sir *Robert Filmer* tells us, *Observations, A. 55. a liberty for every one to do what he lists, to live as he pleases, and not to be tied by any laws:* but *freedom of men under government* is, to have a standing rule to live by, common to every one of that society, and made by the legislative power erected in it; a liberty to follow my own will in all things, where the rule prescribes not; and not to be subject to the inconstant, uncertain, unknown, arbitrary will of another man: as *freedom of nature* is, to be under no other restraint but the law of nature.

§. 23. This *freedom* from absolute, arbitrary power, is so necessary to, and closely joined with a man's preservation, that he cannot part with it, but by what forfeits his preservation and life together: for a man, not having the power of his own life, *cannot*, by compact, or his own consent, *enslave himself* to any one, nor put himself under the absolute, arbitrary power of another, to take away his life, when he pleases. No body can give more power than he has himself, and he that cannot take away his own life, cannot give another power over it. Indeed, having by his fault forfeited his own life, by some act that deserves death; he, to whom he has forfeited it, may (when he has him in his power) delay to take it, and make use of him to his own service, and he does him no injury by it: for, whenever he finds the hardship of his slavery outweigh the value of his life, it is in his power, by resisting the will of his master, to draw on himself the death he desires.

§. 24. This is the perfect condition of *slavery*, which is nothing else, but *the state of war continued, between a lawful conqueror and a captive:* for, if once *compact* enter between them, and make an agreement for a limited power on the one side, and obedience on the other, the *state of war and slavery* ceases, as long as the compact endures: for, as has been said, no man can, by agreement, pass over to another that which he hath not in himself, a power over his own life.

I confess, we find among the *Jews*, as well as other nations, that men did sell themselves; but, it is plain, this was only to *drudgery*, *not to slavery:* for, it is evident, the person sold was not under an absolute, arbitrary, despotical power: for the master could not have power to kill him, at any time, whom, at a certain time, he was obliged to let go free out of his service; and the master of such a servant was so far from having an arbitrary power over his life, that he could not, at pleasure, so much as maim him, but the loss of an eye, or tooth, set him free, *Exod.* xxi.

CHAP. V.
Of PROPERTY.

§. 25. Whether we consider natural *reason*, which tells us, that men, being once born, have a right to their preservation, and consequently to meat and drink, and such other things as nature affords for their subsistence: or *revelation*, which gives us an account of those grants God made of the world to *Adam*, and to *Noah*, and his sons, it is very clear, that God, as king *David* says, *Psal.* cxv. 16. *has given the earth to the children of men;* given it to mankind in common. But this being supposed, it seems to some a very great difficulty, how any one should ever come to have a *property* in any thing: I will not content myself to answer, that if it be difficult to make out *property*, upon a supposition that God gave the world to *Adam*, and his posterity in common, it is impossible that any man, but one universal monarch, should have any *property* upon a supposition, that God gave the world to *Adam*, and his heirs in succession, exclusive of all the rest of his posterity. But I shall endeavour to shew, how men might come to have a *property* in several parts of that which God gave to mankind in common, and that without any express compact of all the commoners.

§. 26. God, who hath given the world to men in common, hath also given them reason to make use of it to the best advantage of life, and convenience. The earth, and all that is therein, is given to men for the support and comfort of their being. And tho' all the fruits it naturally produces, and beasts it feeds, belong to mankind in common, as they are produced by the spontaneous hand of nature; and no body has originally a private dominion, exclusive of the rest of mankind, in any of them, as they are thus in their natural state: yet being given for the use of men, there must of necessity be *a means to appropriate* them some way or other, before they can be of any use, or at all beneficial to any particular man. The fruit, or venison, which nourishes the wild *Indian*, who knows no inclosure, and is still a tenant in common, must be his, and so his, *i. e.* a part of him, that another can no longer have any right to it, before it can do him any good for the support of his life.

§. 27. Though the earth, and all inferior creatures, be common to all men, yet every man has a *property* in his own *person:* this no body has any right to but himself. The *labour* of his body, and the *work* of his hands, we may say, are properly his. Whatsoever then he removes out of the state that nature hath provided, and left it in, he hath mixed his *labour* with, and joined to it something that is his own, and thereby makes it his *property*. It being by him removed from the common state nature hath placed it in, it hath by this *labour* something annexed to it, that excludes the common right of other men: for this *labour* being the unquestionable property of the labourer, no man but he can have a right to what that is once joined to, at least where there is enough, and as good, left in common for others.

§. 28. He that is nourished by the acorns he picked up under an oak, or the apples he gathered from the trees in the wood, has certainly appropriated them to himself. No body can deny but the nourishment is his. I ask then, when did they begin to be his? when he digested? or when he eat? or when he boiled? or when he brought them home? or when he picked them up? and it is plain, if the first gathering made them not his, nothing else could. That *labour* put a distinction between them and common: that added something to them more than nature, the common mother of all, had done; and so they became his private right. And will any one say, he had no right to those acorns or apples, he thus appropriated, because he had not the consent of all mankind to make them his? Was it a robbery thus to assume to himself what belonged to all in common? If such a consent as that was necessary, man had starved, notwithstanding the plenty God had given him. We see in *commons*, which remain so by compact, that it is the taking any part of what is common, and removing it out of the state nature leaves it in, which *begins the property*; without which the common is of no use. And the taking of this or that part, does not depend on the express consent of all the commoners. Thus the grass my horse has bit; the turfs my servant has cut; and the ore I have digged in any place, where I have a right to them in common with others, become my *property*, without the assignation or consent of any body. The *labour* that was mine, removing them out of that common state they were in, hath *fixed* my *property* in them.

§. 29. By making an explicit consent of every commoner, necessary to any one's appropriating to himself any part of what is given in common, children or servants could not cut the meat, which their father or master had provided for them in common, without assigning to every one his peculiar part. Though the water running in the fountain be every one's, yet who can doubt, but that in the pitcher is his only who drew it out? His *labour* hath taken it out of the hands of nature, where it was common, and belonged equally to all her children, and *hath* thereby *appropriated* it to himself.

§. 30. Thus this law of reason makes the deer that *Indian's* who hath killed it; it is allowed to be his goods, who hath bestowed his labour upon it, though before it was the common right of every one. And amongst those who are counted the civilized part of mankind, who have made and multiplied positive laws to determine *property*, this original law of nature, for the *beginning of property*, in what was before common, still takes place; and by virtue thereof, what fish any one catches in the ocean, that great and still remaining common of mankind; or what ambergrise any one takes up here, is by the *labour* that removes it out of that common state nature left it in, *made* his *property*, who takes that pains about it. And even amongst us, the hare that any one is hunting, is thought his who pursues her during the chase: for being a beast that is still looked upon as common, and no man's private possession; whoever has employed so much *labour* about any of that kind, as to find and pursue her, has thereby removed her from the state of nature, wherein she was common, and hath *begun a property*.

§. 31. It will perhaps be objected to this, that if gathering the acorns, or other fruits of the earth, &c. makes a right to them, then any one may *ingross* as much as he will. To which I answer, Not so. The same law of nature, that does by this means give us property, does also *bound* that *property* too. *God has given us all things richly*, 1 Tim. vi. 12. is the voice of reason confirmed by inspiration. But how far has he given it us? *To enjoy*. As much as any one can make use of to any advantage of life before it spoils, so much he may by his labour fix a property in: whatever is beyond this, is more than his share, and belongs to others. Nothing was made by God for man to spoil or destroy. And thus, considering the plenty of natural provisions there was a long time in the world, and the few spenders; and to how small a part of that provision the industry of one man could extend itself, and ingross it to the prejudice of others; especially keeping within the *bounds*, set by reason, of what might serve for his *use;* there could be then little room for quarrels or contentions about property so established.

§. 32. But the *chief matter of property* being now not the fruits of the earth, and the beasts that subsist on it, but *the earth itself;* as that which takes in and carries with it all the rest; I think it is plain, that *property* in that too is acquired as the former. *As much land* as a man tills, plants, improves, cultivates, and can use the product of, so much is his *property.* He by his labour does, as it were, inclose it from the common. Nor will it invalidate his right, to say every body else has an equal title to it; and therefore he cannot appropriate, he cannot inclose, without the consent of all his fellow-commoners, all mankind. God, when he gave the world in common to all mankind, commanded man also to labour, and the penury of his condition required it of him. God and his reason commanded him to subdue the earth, *i. e.* improve it for the benefit of life, and therein lay out something upon it that was his own, his labour. He that in obedience to this command of God, subdued, tilled and sowed any part of it, thereby annexed to it something that was his *property,* which another had no title to, nor could without injury take from him.

§. 33. Nor was this *appropriation* of any parcel of *land*, by improving it, any prejudice to any other man, since there was still enough, and as good left; and more than the yet unprovided could use. So that, in effect, there was never the less left for others because of his inclosure for himself: for he that leaves as much as another can make use of, does as good as take nothing at all. No body could think himself injured by the drinking of another man, though he took a good draught, who had a whole river of the same water left him to quench his thirst: and the case of land and water, where there is enough of both, is perfectly the same.

§. 34. God gave the world to men in common; but since he gave it them for their benefit, and the greatest conveniencies of life they were capable to draw from it, it cannot be supposed he meant it should always remain common and uncultivated. He gave it to the use of the industrious and rational, (and *labour* was to be *his title* to it;) not to the fancy or covetousness of the quarrelsome and conten-

tious. He that had as good left for his improvement, as was already
taken up, needed not complain, ought not to meddle with what was
already improved by another's labour: if he did, it is plain he
desired the benefit of another's pains, which he had no right to, and
not the ground which God had given him in common with others to
labour on, and whereof there was as good left, as that already
possessed, and more than he knew what to do with, or his industry
could reach to.

§. 35. It is true, in *land* that is *common* in *England,* or any other
country, where there is plenty of people under government, who
have money and commerce, no one can inclose or appropriate any
part, without the consent of all his fellow-commoners; because this
is left common by compact, *i. e.* by the law of the land, which is not
to be violated. And though it be common, in respect of some men,
it is not so to all mankind; but is the joint property of this country,
or this parish. Besides, the remainder, after such inclosure, would
not be as good to the rest of the commoners, as the whole was when
they could all make use of the whole; whereas in the beginning and
first peopling of the great common of the world, it was quite otherwise. The law man was under, was rather for appropriating. God
commanded, and his wants forced him to *labour.* That was his *property* which could not be taken from him where-ever he had fixed
it. And hence subduing or cultivating the earth, and having dominion, we see are joined together. The one gave title to the other. So
that God, by commanding to subdue, gave authority so far to *appropriate:* and the condition of human life, which requires labour
and materials to work on, necessarily introduces private possessions.

§. 36. The *measure of property* nature has well set by the extent
of men's *labour and the conveniencies of life:* no man's labour could
subdue, or appropriate all; nor could his enjoyment consume more
than a small part; so that it was impossible for any man, this way,
to intrench upon the right of another, or acquire to himself a property, to the prejudice of his neighbour, who would still have room
for as good, and as large a possession (after the other had taken out
his) as before it was appropriated. This *measure* did confine every
man's *possession* to a very moderate proportion, and such as he
might appropriate to himself, without injury to any body, in the
first ages of the world, when men were more in danger to be lost, by
wandering from their company, in the then vast wilderness of the
earth, than to be straitened for want of room to plant in. And the

same *measure* may be allowed still without prejudice to any body, as full as the world seems: for supposing a man, or family, in the state they were at first peopling of the world by the children of *Adam*, or *Noah*; let him plant in some in-land, vacant places of *America*, we shall find that the *possessions* he could make himself, upon the *measures* we have given, would not be very large, nor, even to this day, prejudice the rest of mankind, or give them reason to complain, or think themselves injured by this man's incroach-ment, though the race of men have now spread themselves to all the corners of the world, and do infinitely exceed the small number was at the beginning. Nay, the extent of *ground* is of so little value, *without labour*, that I have heard it affirmed, that in *Spain* itself a man may be permitted to plough, sow and reap, without being disturbed, upon land he has no other title to, but only his making use of it. But, on the contrary, the inhabitants think themselves beholden to him, who, by his industry on neglected, and conse-quently waste land, has increased the stock of corn, which they wanted. But be this as it will, which I lay no stress on; this I dare boldly affirm, that the same *rule of propriety*, *(viz.)* that every man should have as much as he could make use of, would hold still in the world, without straitening any body; since there is land enough in the world to suffice double the inhabitants, had not the *invention of money*, and the tacit agreement of men to put a value on it, in-troduced (by consent) larger possessions, and a right to them; which, how it has done, I shall by and by shew more at large.

§. 37. This is certain, that in the beginning, before the desire of having more than man needed had altered the intrinsic value of things, which depends only on their usefulness to the life of man; or had *agreed, that a little piece of yellow metal*, which would keep without wasting or decay, should be worth a great piece of flesh, or a whole heap of corn; though men had a right to appropriate, by their labour, each one of himself, as much of the things of nature, as he could use: yet this could not be much, nor to the prejudice of others, where the same plenty was still left to those who would use the same industry. To which let me add, that he who appropriates land to himself by his labour, does not lessen, but increase the com-mon stock of mankind: for the provisions serving to the support of human life, produced by one acre of inclosed and cultivated land, are (to speak much within compass) ten times more than those which are yielded by an acre of land of an equal richness lying waste in common. And therefore he that incloses land, and has a greater

plenty of the conveniencies of life from ten acres, than he could
have from an hundred left to nature, may truly be said to give nine-
ty acres to mankind: for his labour now supplies him with provisions out of ten acres, which were but the product of an hundred lying in common. I have here rated the improved land very low, in
making its product but as ten to one, when it is much nearer an hundred to one: for I ask, whether in the wild woods and uncultivated
waste of *America*, left to nature, without any improvement, tillage
or husbandry, a thousand acres yield the needy and wretched inhabitants as many conveniencies of life, as ten acres of equally fer-
tile land do in *Devonshire*, where they are well cultivated?

Before the appropriation of land, he who gathered as much of the
wild fruit, killed, caught, or tamed, as many of the beasts, as he
could; he that so imployed his pains about any of the spontaneous
products of nature, as any way to alter them from the state which
nature put them in, *by* placing any of his *labour* on them, did
thereby *acquire a propriety in them:* but if they perished, in his
possession, without their due use; if the fruits rotted, or the venison
putrified, before he could spend it, he offended against the common
law of nature, and was liable to be punished; he invaded his
neighbour's share, for he had *no right, farther than his use* called for
any of them, and they might serve to afford him conveniencies of
life.

§. 38. The same *measures* governed the *possession of land* too:
whatsoever he tilled and reaped, laid up and made use of, before it
spoiled, that was his peculiar right; whatsoever he enclosed, and
could feed, and make use of, the cattle and product was also his.
But if either the grass of his inclosure rotted on the ground, or the
fruit of his planting perished without gathering, and laying up, this
part of the earth, notwithstanding his inclosure, was still to be
looked on as waste, and might be the possession of any other. Thus,
at the beginning, *Cain* might take as much ground as he could till,
and make it his own land, and yet leave enough to *Abel's* sheep to
feed on; a few acres would serve for both their possessions. But as
families increased, and industry inlarged their stocks, their *possessions inlarged* with the need of them; but yet it was commonly
without any fixed property in the ground they made use of, till they
incorporated, settled themselves together, and built cities; and then,
by consent, they came in time, to set out the *bounds of their distinct
territories,* and agree on limits between them and their neighbours;
and by laws within themselves, settled the *properties* of those of the

same society: for we see, that in that part of the world which was
first inhabited, and therefore like to be best peopled, even as low
down as *Abraham's* time, they wandered with their flocks, and
their herds, which was their substance, freely up and down; and this
Abraham did, in a country where he was a stranger. Whence it is
plain, that at least a great part of the *land lay in common;* that the
inhabitants valued it not, nor claimed property in any more than
they made use of. But when there was not room enough in the same
place, for their herds to feed together, they by consent, as *Abraham*
and *Lot* did, *Gen.* xiii. 5. separated and inlarged their pasture,
where it best liked them. And for the same reason *Esau* went from
his father, and his brother, and planted in *mount Seir, Gen.* xxxvi.
6.

§. 39. And thus, without supposing any private dominion, and
property in *Adam,* over all the world, exclusive of all other men,
which can no way be proved, nor any one's property be made out
from it; but supposing the *world* given, as it was, to the children of
men *in common,* we see how *labour* could make men distinct titles
to several parcels of it, for their private uses; wherein there could be
no doubt of right, no room for quarrel.

§. 40. Nor is it so strange, as perhaps before consideration it may
appear, that the *property of labour* should be able to over-balance
the community of land: for it is *labour* indeed that *puts the difference of value* on every thing; and let any one consider what the
difference is between an acre of land planted with tobacco or sugar,
sown with wheat or barley, and an acre of the same land lying in
common, without any husbandry upon it, and he will find, that the
improvement of *labour makes* the far greater part of the value. I
think it will be but a very modest computation to say, that of the
products of the earth useful to the life of man nine tenths are the *effects of labour:* nay, if we will rightly estimate things as they come
to our use, and cast up the several expences about them, what in
them is purely owing to *nature,* and what to *labour,* we shall find,
that in most of them ninety-nine hundredths are wholly to be put on
the account of *labour.*

§. 41. There cannot be a clearer demonstration of any thing, than
several nations of the *Americans* are of this, who are rich in land,
and poor in all the comforts of life; whom nature having furnished
as liberally as any other people, with the materials of plenty, *i. e.* a
fruitful soil, apt to produce in abundance, what might serve for
food, raiment, and delight; yet for *want of improving it by labour,*

have not one hundredth part of the conveniencies we enjoy: and a king of a large and fruitful territory there, feeds, lodges, and is clad worse than a day-labourer in *England*.

§. 42. To make this a little clearer, let us but trace some of the ordinary provisions of life, through their several progresses, before they come to our use, and see how much they receive of their *value from human industry*. Bread, wine and cloth, are things of daily use, and great plenty; yet notwithstanding, acorns, water and leaves, or skins, must be our bread, drink and cloathing, did not *labour* furnish us with these more useful commodities: for whatever *bread* is more worth than acorns, wine than water, and *cloth* or *silk*, than leaves, skins or moss, that is wholly *owing to labour* and *industry*; the one of these being the food and raiment which unassisted nature furnishes us with; the other, provisions which our industry and pains prepare for us, which how much they exceed the other in value, when any one hath computed, he will then see how much *labour makes the far greatest part of the value* of things we enjoy in this world: and the ground which produces the materials, is scarce to be reckoned in, as any, or at most, but a very small part of it; so little, that even amongst us, land that is left wholly to nature, that hath no improvement of pasturage, tillage, or planting, is called, as indeed it is, *waste*; and we shall find the benefit of it amount to little more than nothing.

This shews how much numbers of men are to be preferred to largeness of dominions; and that the increase of lands, and the right employing of them, is the great art of government: and that prince, who shall be so wise and godlike, as by established laws of liberty to secure protection and encouragement to the honest industry of mankind, against the oppression of power and narrowness of party, will quickly be too hard for his neighbours: but this by the by. To return to the argument in hand,

§. 43. An acre of land, that bears here twenty bushels of wheat, and another in *America*, which, with the same husbandry, would do the like, are, without doubt, of the same natural intrinsic value: but yet the benefit mankind receives from the one in a year, is worth 5*l*. and from the other possibly not worth a penny, if all the profit an *Indian* received from it were to be valued, and sold here; at least, I may truly say, not one thousandth. It is *labour* then which *puts the greatest part of value upon land*, without which it would scarcely be worth any thing: it is to that we owe the greatest part of all its useful products; for all that the straw, bran, bread, of that

acre of wheat, is more worth than the product of an acre of as good
land, which lies waste, is all the effect of labour: for it is not barely
the plough-man's pains, the reaper's and thresher's toil, and the
baker's sweat, is to be counted into the *bread* we eat; the labour of
those who broke the oxen, who digged and wrought the iron and
stones, who felled and framed the timber employed about the
plough, mill, oven, or any other utensils, which are a vast number,
requisite to this corn, from its being feed to be sown to its being
made bread, must all be *charged on* the account of labour, and
received as an effect of that: nature and the earth furnished only the
almost worthless materials, as in themselves. It would be a strange
*catalogue of things, that industry provided and made use of, about
every loaf of bread,* before it came to our use, if we could trace
them; iron, wood, leather, bark, timber, stone, bricks, coals, lime,
cloth, dying drugs, pitch, tar, masts, ropes, and all the materials
made use of in the ship, that brought any of the commodities made
use of by any of the workmen, to any part of the work; all which it
would be almost impossible, at least too long, to reckon up.

§. 44. From all which it is evident, that though the things of
nature are given in common, yet man, by being master of himself,
and *proprietor of his own person, and the actions or labour of it,
had still in himself the great foundation of property;* and that,
which made up the great part of what he applied to the support or
comfort of his being, when invention and arts had improved the
conveniencies of life, was perfectly his own, and did not belong in
common to others.

§. 45. Thus *labour,* in the beginning, *gave a right of property,*
wherever any one was pleased to employ it upon what was common, which remained a long while the far greater part, and is yet
more than mankind makes use of. Men, at first, for the most part,
contented themselves with what unassisted nature offered to their
necessities: and though afterwards, in some parts of the world,
(where the increase of people and stock, with the *use of money,* had
made land scarce, and so of some value) the several *communities*
settled the bounds of their distinct territories, and by laws within
themselves regulated the properties of the private men of their society, and so, *by compact* and agreement, *settled the property* which
labour and industry began; and the leagues that have been made between several states and kingdoms, either expresly or tacitly dis-
owning all claim and right to the land in the others possession,
have, by common consent, given up their pretences to their natural

common right, which originally they had to those countries, and so have, by *positive agreement, settled a property* amongst themselves, in distinct parts and parcels of the earth; yet there are still *great tracts of ground* to be found, which (the inhabitants thereof not having joined with the rest of mankind, in the consent of the use of their common money) *lie waste*, and are more than the people who dwell on it do, or can make use of, and so still lie in common; tho' this can scarce happen amongst that part of mankind that have consented to the use of money.

§. 46. The greatest part of *things really useful* to the life of man, and such as the necessity of subsisting made the first commoners of the world look after, as it doth the *Americans* now, *are* generally things of *short duration*; such as, if they are not consumed by use, will decay and perish of themselves: gold, silver and diamonds, are things that fancy or agreement hath put the value on, more than real use, and the necessary support of life. Now of those good things which nature hath provided in common, every one had a right (as hath been said) to as much as he could use, and *property* in all that he could effect with his labour; all that his *industry* could extend to, to alter from the state nature had put it in, was his. He that *gathered* a hundred bushels of acorns or apples, had thereby a *property* in them, they were his goods as soon as gathered. He was only to look, that he used them before they spoiled, else he took more than his share, and robbed others. And indeed it was a foolish thing, as well as dishonest, to hoard up more than he could make use of. If he gave away a part to any body else, so that it perished not uselesly in his possession, these he also made use of. And if he also bartered away plums, that would have rotted in a week, for nuts that would last good for his eating a whole year, he did no injury; he wasted not the common stock; destroyed no part of the portion of goods that belonged to others, so long as nothing perished uselesly in his hands. Again, if he would give his nuts for a piece of metal, pleased with its colour; or exchange his sheep for shells, or wool for a sparkling pebble or a diamond, and keep those by him all his life, he invaded not the right of others, he might heap up as much of these durable things as he pleased; the *exceeding of the bounds of* his *just property* not lying in the largeness of his possession, but the perishing of any thing uselesly in it.

§. 47. And thus *came in the use of money*, some lasting thing that men might keep without spoiling, and that by mutual consent men would take in exchange for the truly useful, but perishable supports of life.

§. 48. And as different degrees of industry were apt to give men possessions in different proportions, so this *invention of money* gave them the opportunity to continue and enlarge them: for supposing an island, separate from all possible commerce with the rest of the world, wherein there were but an hundred families, but there were sheep, horses and cows, with other useful animals, wholsome fruits, and land enough for corn for a hundred thousand times as many, but nothing in the island, either because of its commonness, or perishableness, fit to supply the place of *money*; what reason could any one have there to enlarge his possessions beyond the use of his family, and a plentiful supply to its *consumption*, either in what their own industry produced, or they could barter for like perishable, useful commodities, with others? Where there is not some thing, both lasting and scarce, and so valuable to be hoarded up, there men will not be apt to enlarge their *possessions of land*, were it never so rich, never so free for them to take: for I ask, what would a man value ten thousand, or an hundred thousand acres of excellent *land*, ready cultivated, and well stocked too with cattle, in the middle of the inland parts of *America*, where he had no hopes of commerce with other parts of the world, to draw *money* to him by the sale of the product? It would not be worth the inclosing, and we should see him give up again to the wild common of nature, whatever was more than would supply the conveniencies of life to be had there for him and his family.

§. 49. Thus in the beginning all the world was *America*, and more so than that is now; for no such thing as *money* was any where known. Find out something that hath the *use and value of money* amongst his neighbours, you shall see the same man will begin presently to enlarge his possessions.

§. 50. But since gold and silver, being little useful to the life of man in proportion to food, raiment, and carriage, has its *value* only from the consent of men, whereof *labour* yet *makes*, in great part, *the measure*, it is plain, that men have agreed to a disproportionate and unequal *possession of the earth*, they having, by a tacit and voluntary consent, found out a way how a man may fairly possess more land than he himself can use the product of, by receiving in exchange for the overplus gold and silver, which may be hoarded up without injury to any one; these metals not spoiling or decaying in the hands of the possessor. This partage of things in an inequality of private possessions, men have made practicable out of the bounds of society, and without compact, only by putting a value on gold

and silver, and tacitly agreeing in the use of money: for in governments, the laws regulate the right of property, and the possession of
land is determined by positive constitutions.

§. 51. And thus, I think, it is very easy to conceive, without any
difficulty, *how labour could at first begin a title of property* in the
common things of nature, and how the spending it upon our uses
bounded it. So that there could then be no reason of quarrelling
about title, nor any doubt about the largeness of possession it gave.
Right and conveniency went together; for as a man had a right to all
he could employ his labour upon, so he had no temptation to
labour for more than he could make use of. This left no room for
controversy about the title, nor for incroachment on the right of
others; what portion a man carved to himself, was easily seen; and
it was useless, as well as dishonest, to carve himself too much, or
take more than he needed.

CHAP. VI.
Of Paternal Power.

§. 52. IT may perhaps be censured as an impertinent criticism, in a
discourse of this nature, to find fault with words and names, that
have obtained in the world: and yet possibly it may not be amiss to
offer new ones, when the old are apt to lead men into mistakes, as
this of *paternal power* probably has done, which seems so to place
the power of parents over their children wholly in the *father*, as if
the *mother* had no share in it; whereas, if we consult reason or
revelation, we shall find, she hath an equal title. This may give one
reason to ask, whether this might not be more properly called
parental power? for whatever obligation nature and the right of
generation lays on children, it must certainly bind them equal to
both the concurrent causes of it. And accordingly we see the
positive law of God every where joins them together, without
distinction, when it commands the obedience of children, *Honour
thy father and thy mother,* Exod. xx. 12. *Whosoever curseth his
father or his mother,* Lev. xx. 9. *Ye shall fear every man his mother
and his father,* Lev. xix. 3. *Children, obey your parents,* &c. Eph.
vi. 1. is the stile of the Old and New Testament.

§. 53. Had but this one thing been well considered, without looking any deeper into the matter, it might perhaps have kept men
from running into those gross mistakes, they have made, about this

power of parents; which, however it might, without any great
harshness, bear the name of absolute dominion, and regal authority, when under the title of *paternal power* it seemed appropriated to
the father, would yet have founded but oddly, and in the very name
shewn the absurdity, if this supposed absolute power over children
had been called *parental;* and thereby have discovered, that it
belonged to the *mother* too: for it will but very ill serve the turn of
those men, who contend so much for the absolute power and
authority of the *fatherhood*, as they call it, that the mother should
have any share in it; and it would have but ill supported the *monarchy* they contend for, when by the very name it appeared, that
that fundamental authority, from whence they would derive their
government of a single person only, was not placed in one, but two
persons jointly. But to let this of names pass.

§. 54. Though I have said above, *Chap. II. That all men by
nature are equal*, I cannot be supposed to understand all sorts of
equality: age or *virtue* may give men a just precedency: *excellency
of parts* and *merit* may place others above the common level: *birth*
may subject some, and *alliance* or *benefits* others, to pay an obser-
vance to those to whom nature, gratitude, or other respects, may
have made it due: and yet all this consists with the *equality*, which
all men are in, in respect of jurisdiction or dominion one over
another; which was the *equality* I there spoke of, as proper to the
business in hand, being that *equal right*, that every man hath, *to his
natural freedom*, without being subjected to the will or authority of
any other man.

§. 55. *Children*, I confess, are not born in this full state of *equality*, though they are born to it. Their parents have a sort of rule and
jurisdiction over them, when they come into the world, and for
some time after; but it is but a temporary one. The bonds of this
subjection are like the swaddling clothes they art wrapt up in, and
supported by, in the weakness of their infancy: age and reason as
they grow up, loosen them, till at length they drop quite off, and
leave a man at his own free disposal.

§. 56. *Adam* was created a perfect man, his body and mind in full
possession of their strength and reason, and so was capable, from
the first instant of his being to provide for his own support and
preservation, and govern his actions according to the dictates of the
law of reason which God had implanted in him. From him the
world is peopled with his descendants, who are all born infants,
weak and helpless, without knowledge or understanding: but to

supply the defects of this imperfect state, till the improvement of growth and age hath removed them, *Adam* and *Eve*, and after them all *parents* were, by the law of nature, *under an obligation to preserve, nourish, and educate the children* they had begotten; not as their own workmanship, but the workmanship of their own maker, the Almighty, to whom they were to be accountable for them.

§. 57. The law, that was to govern *Adam*, was the same that was to govern all his posterity, the *law of reason*. But his offspring having another way of entrance into the world, different from him, by a natural birth, that produced them ignorant and without the use of *reason*, they were not presently *under that law*; for no body can be under a law, which is not promulgated to him; and this law being promulgated or made known by *reason* only, he that is not come to the use of his *reason*, cannot be said to be *under this law*; and *Adam*'s children, being not presently as soon as born *under this law of reason*, were not presently *free*: for *law*, in its true notion, *is* not so much the limitation as *the direction of a free and intelligent agent* to his proper interest, and prescribes no farther than is for the general good of those under that law: could they be happier without it, the *law*, as an useless thing, would of itself vanish; and that ill deserves the name of confinement which hedges us in only from bogs and precipices. So that, however it may be mistaken, *the end of law is* not to abolish or restrain, but *to preserve and enlarge freedom*: for in all the states of created beings capable of laws, *where there is no law, there is no freedom*: for *liberty* is, to be free from restraint and violence from others; which cannot be, where there is no law: but freedom is not, as we are told, *a liberty for every man to do what he lists*: (for who could be free, when every other man's humour might domineer over him?) but a *liberty* to dispose, and order as he lists, his person, actions, possessions, and his whole property, within the allowance of those laws under which he is, and therein not to be subject to the arbitrary will of another, but freely follow his own.

§. 58. The *power*, then, *that parents have* over their children, arises from that duty which is incumbent on them, to take care of their off-spring, during the imperfect state of childhood. To inform the mind, and govern the actions of their yet ignorant nonage, till reason shall take its place, and ease them of that trouble, is what the children want, and the parents are bound to: for God having given man an understanding to direct his actions, has allowed him a freedom of will, and liberty of acting, as properly belonging thereunto, within the bounds of that law he is under. But whilst he is in an estate, wherein he has not *understanding* of his own to direct his *will*, he is not to have any *will* of his own to follow: he that *understands* for him, must *will* for him too; he must prescribe to his will, and regulate his actions; but when he comes to the estate that made his *father a freeman, the son is a freeman* too.

§. 59. This holds in all the laws a man is under, whether natural or civil. Is a man under the law of nature? *What made him free* of that law? what gave him a free disposing of his property, according to his own will, within the compass of that law? I answer, a state of maturity wherein he might be supposed capable to know that law, that so he might keep his actions within the bounds of it. When he has acquired that state, he is presumed to know how far that law is to be his guide, and how far he may make use of his *freedom*, and so comes to have it; till then, some body else must guide him, who is presumed to know how far the law allows a liberty. If such a state of reason, such an age of discretion *made him free*, the same shall make his son free too. Is a man under the law of *England?* *What made him free* of that law? that is, to have the liberty to dispose of his actions and possessions according to his own will, within the permission of that law? A capacity of knowing that law; which is supposed by that law, at the age of one and twenty years, and in some cases sooner. If this *made* the father *free*, it shall *make* the son *free* too. Till then we see the law allows the son to have no will, but he is to be guided by the will of his father or guardian, who is to understand for him. And if the father die, and fail to substitute a deputy in his trust; if he hath not provided a tutor, to govern his son, during his minority, during his want of understanding, the law takes care to do it; some other must govern him, and be a will to him, till he hath *attained to a state of freedom*, and his understanding be fit to take the government of his will. But after that, the father and son are equally *free* as much as tutor and pupil after nonage; equally subjects of the same law together, without any dominion left in the father over the life, liberty, or estate of his son, whether they be only in the state and under the law of nature, or under the positive laws of an established government.

§. 60. But if, through defects that may happen out of the ordinary course of nature, any one comes not to such a degree of reason, wherein he might be supposed capable of knowing the law, and so living within the rules of it, he is *never capable of being a free man*, he is never let loose to the disposure of his own will (because he knows no bounds to it, has not understanding, its proper guide) but is continued under the tuition and government of others, all the time his own understanding is uncapable of that charge. And so *lunatics* and *ideots* are never set free from the government of their parents; *children, who are not as yet come unto those years whereat they may have; and innocents which are excluded by a natural defect from ever having;* thirdly, *madmen, which for the present cannot possibly have the use of right reason to guide themselves, have for their guide, the reason that guideth other men which are tutors over them, to seek and procure their good for them, says* Hooker, Eccl. Pol. *lib.* i. *sect.* 7. All which seems no more than that duty, which God and nature has laid on man, as well as other creatures, to preserve their offspring, till they can be able to shift for themselves, and will scarce amount to an instance or proof of *parents* regal authority.

§. 61. Thus we are *born free*, as we are born rational; not that we have actually the exercise of either: age, that brings one, brings with it the other too. And thus we see how *natural freedom and subjection to parents* may consist together, and are both founded on the same principle. A *child* is *free* by his father's title, by his father's understanding, which is to govern him till he hath it of his own. The *freedom of a man at years of discretion*, and the *subjection* of a child *to* his *parents*, whilst yet short of that age, are so consistent, and so distinguishable, that the most blinded contenders for monarchy, *by right of fatherhood*, cannot miss this *difference*; the most obstinate cannot but allow their consistency: for were their doctrine all true, were the right heir of *Adam* now known, and by that title settled a monarch in his throne, invested with all the absolute unlimited power Sir *Robert Filmer* talks of; if he should die as soon as his heir were born, must not the *child*, notwithstanding he were never so free, never so much sovereign, be in subjection to his mother and nurse, to tutors and governors, till age and education brought him reason and ability to govern himself and others? The necessities of his life, the health of his body, and the information of his mind, would require him to be directed by the will of others, and not his own; and yet will any one think, that this restraint and subjection were inconsistent with, or spoiled him of that liberty or sovereignty he had a right to, or gave away his empire to those who had the government of his nonage? This government over him only prepared him the better and sooner for it. If any body should ask

me, when my son is *of age to be free?* I shall answer, just when his
monarch is of age to govern. *But at what time,* says the judicious
Hooker, Eccl. Pol. l. i. sect. 6. *u mun may be said to have attained
so far forth the use of reason, as sufficeth to make him capable of
those laws whereby he is then bound to guide his actions: this is a
great deal more easy for sense to discern, than for any one by skill
and learning to determine.*

§. 62. Common-wealths themselves take notice of, and allow,
that there is a *time when men* are to *begin to act like free men,* and
therefore till that time require not oaths of fealty, or allegiance, or
other public owning of, or submission to the government of their
countries.

§. 63. The *freedom* then of man, and liberty of acting according
to his own will, is *grounded on* his having *reason,* which is able to
instruct him in that law he is to govern himself by, and make him
know how far he is left to the freedom of his own will. To turn him
loose to an unrestrained liberty, before he has reason to guide him,
is not the allowing him the privilege of his nature to be free; but to
thrust him out amongst brutes, and abandon him to a state as
wretched, and as much beneath that of a man, as their's. This is that
which puts the *authority* into the *parents* hands to govern the
minority of their children. God hath made it their business to
employ this care on their offspring, and hath placed in them suitable
inclinations of tenderness and concern to temper this power, to ap-
ply it, as his wisdom designed it, to the children's good, as long as
they should need to be under it.

§. 64. But what reason can hence advance this care of the *parents*
due to their off-spring into an *absolute arbitrary dominion* of the
father, whose power reaches no farther, than by such a discipline,
as he finds most effectual, to give such strength and health to their
bodies, such vigour and rectitude to their minds, as may best fit his
children to be most useful to themselves and others; and, if it be
necessary to his condition, to make them work, when they are able,
for their own subsistence. But in this power the *mother* too has her
share with the *father.*

§. 65. Nay, this *power* so little belongs to the *father* by any
peculiar right of nature, but only as he is guardian of his children,
that when he quits his care of them, he loses his power over them,
which goes along with their nourishment and education, to which it
is inseparably annexed; and it belongs as much to the *foster-father*
of an exposed child, as to the natural father of another. So little

power does the bare *act of begetting* give a man over his issue; if all
his care ends there, and this be all the title he hath to the name and
authority of a father. And what will become of this *paternal power*
in that part of the world, where one woman hath more than one
husband at a time? or in those parts of *America,* where, when the
husband and wife part, which happens frequently, the children are
all left to the mother, follow her, and are wholly under her care and
provision? If the father die whilst the children are young, do they
not naturally every where owe the same obedience to their *mother,*
during their minority, as to their father were he alive? and will any
one say, that the mother hath a legislative power over her children?
that she can make standing rules, which shall be of perpetual obligation, by which they ought to regulate all the concerns of their property, and bound their liberty all the course of their lives? or can she
inforce the observation of them with capital punishments? for this is
the proper *power of the magistrate,* of which the father hath not so
much as the shadow. His command over his children is but temporary, and reaches not their life or property: it is but a help to the
weakness and imperfection of their nonage, a discipline necessary to
their education: and though a *father* may dispose of his own possessions as he pleases, when his children are out of danger of perishing
for want, yet *his power* extends not to the lives or goods, which
either their own industry, or another's bounty has made their's; nor
to their liberty neither, when they are once arrived to the infran-
chisement of the years of discretion. The *father's empire* then
ceases, and he can from thence forwards no more dispose of the
liberty of his son, than that of any other man: and it must be far
from an absolute or perpetual jurisdiction, from which a man may
withdraw himself, having license from divine authority to *leave
father and mother, and cleave to his wife.*

§. 66. But though there be a time when a *child* comes to be as *free*
from subjection to the will and command of his father, as the father
himself is free from subjection to the will of any body else, and they
are each under no other restraint, but that which is common to
them both, whether it be the law of nature, or municipal law of
their country; yet this freedom exempts not a son from that *honour*
which he ought, by the law of God and nature, *to* pay his *parents.*
God having made the parents instruments in his great design of con-
tinuing the race of mankind, and the occasions of life to their
children; as he hath laid on them an obligation to nourish, preserve,
and bring up their offspring; so he has laid on the children a

perpetual obligation of *honouring their parents*, which containing
in it an inward esteem and reverence to be shewn by all outward expressions, ties up the child from any thing that may ever injure or
affront, disturb or endanger, the happiness or life of those from
whom he received his; and engages him in all actions of defence,
relief, assistance and comfort of those, by whose means he entered
into being, and has been made capable of any enjoyments of life:
from this obligation no state, no freedom can absolve children. But
this is very far from giving parents a power of command over their
children, or an authority to make laws and dispose as they please of
their lives or liberties. It is one thing to owe honour, respect,
gratitude and assistance; another to require an absolute obedience
and submission. The *honour due to parents*, a monarch in his
throne owes his mother; and yet this lessens not his authority, nor
subjects him to her government.

§. 67. The subjection of a minor places in the father a temporary
government, which terminates with the minority of the child: and
the *honour due from a child*, places in the parents a perpetual right
to respect, reverence, support and compliance too, more or less, as
the father's care, cost, and kindness in his education, has been more
or less. This ends not with minority, but holds in all parts and conditions of a man's life. The want of distinguishing these two powers,
viz. that which the father hath in the right of *tuition*, during minority, and the right of *honour* all his life, may perhaps have caused a
great part of the mistakes about this matter: for to speak properly of
them, the first of these is rather the privilege of children, and duty
of parents, than any prerogative of paternal power. The nourishment and education of their children is a charge so incumbent on
parents for their children's good, that nothing can absolve them
from taking care of it: and though the *power of commanding and
chastising* them go along with it, yet God hath woven into the principles of human nature such a tenderness for their off-spring, that
there is little fear that parents should use their power with too much
rigour; the excess is seldom on the severe side, the strong byass of
nature drawing the other way. And therefore God almighty when
he would express his gentle dealing with the *Israelites*, he tells them,
that though he chastened them, *he chastened them as a man
chastens his son*, Deut. viii. 5. *i. e.* with tenderness and affection,
and kept them under no severer discipline than what was absolutely
best for them, and had been less kindness to have slackened. This is
that power to which *children* are commanded *obedience*, that the

pains and care of their parents may not be increased, or ill rewarded.

§. 68. On the other side, *honour* and *support*, all that which gratitude requires to return for the benefits received by and from them, is the indispensible duty of the child, and the proper privilege of the parents. This is intended for the parents advantage, as the other is for the child's; though education, the parents duty, seems to have most power, because the ignorance and infirmities of childhood stand in need of restraint and correction; which is a visible exercise of rule, and a kind of dominion. And that duty which is comprehended in the word *honour*, requires less obedience, though the obligation be stronger on grown, than younger children: for who can think the command, *Children obey your parents*, requires in a man, that has children of his own, the same submission to his father, as it does in his yet young children to him; and that by this precept he were bound to obey all his father's commands, if, out of a conceit of authority, he should have the indiscretion to treat him still as a boy?

§. 69. The first part then of *paternal power*, or rather duty, which is *education*, belongs so to the father, that it terminates at a certain season; when the business of education is over, it ceases of itself, and is also alienable before: for a man may put the tuition of his son in other hands; and he that has made his son an *apprentice* to another, has discharged him, during that time, of a great part of his obedience both to himself and to his mother. But all the *duty of honour*, the other part, remains never the less entire to them; nothing can cancel that: it is so inseparable from them both, that the father's authority cannot dispossess the mother of this right, nor can any man discharge his son from *honouring* her that bore him. But both these are very far from a power to make laws, and inforcing them with penalties, that may reach estate, liberty, limbs and life. The power of commanding ends with nonage; and though, after that, *honour* and respect, support and defence, and whatsoever gratitude can oblige a man to, for the highest benefits he is naturally capable of, be always due from a son to his parents; yet all this puts no scepter into the father's hand, no sovereign power of commanding. He has no dominion over his son's property, or actions; nor any right, that his will should prescribe to his son's in all things; however it may become his son in many things, not very inconvenient to him and his family, to pay a deference to it.

§. 70. A man may owe *honour* and respect to an ancient, or wise
man; defence to his child or friend; relief and support to the dis-
tressed; and gratitude to a benefactor, to such a degree, that all he
has, all he can do, cannot sufficiently pay it: but all these give no
authority, no right to any one, of making laws over him from
whom they are owing. And it is plain, all this is due not only to the
bare title of father; not only because, as has been said, it is owing to
the mother too; but because these obligations to parents, and the
degrees of what is required of children, may be varied by the different care and kindness, trouble and expence, which is often
employed upon one child more than another.

§. 71. This shews the reason how it comes to pass, that *parents in
societies*, where they themselves are subjects, retain a *power over
their children*, and have as much right to their subjection, as those
who are in the state of nature. Which could not possibly be, if all
political power were only paternal, and that in truth they were one
and the same thing: for then, all paternal power being in the prince,
the subject could naturally have none of it. But these two *powers,
political* and *paternal*, are so perfectly distinct and separate; are
built upon so different foundations, and given to so different ends,
that every subject that is a father, has as much a paternal power
over his children, as the prince has over his: and every prince, that
has parents, owes them as much filial duty and obedience, as the
meanest of his subjects do to their's; and can therefore contain not
any part or degree of that kind of dominion, which a prince or
magistrate has over his subject.

§. 72. Though the obligation on the parents to *bring up* their
children, and the obligation on children to *honour* their parents,
contain all the power on the one hand, and submission on the other,
which are proper to this relation, yet there is *another power* ordinarily *in the father*, whereby he has a tie on the obedience of his
children; which tho' it be common to him with other men, yet the
occasions of shewing it, almost constantly happening to fathers in
their private families, and the instances of it elsewhere being rare,
and less taken notice of, it passes in the world for a part of *paternal
jurisdiction*. And this is the power men generally have to *bestow
their estates* on those who please them best; the possession of the
father being the expectation and inheritance of the children, ordinarily in certain proportions, according to the law and custom of
each country; yet it is commonly in the father's power to bestow it
with a more sparing or liberal hand, according as the behaviour of

this or that child hath comported with his will and humour.

§. 73. This is no small tie on the obedience of children: and there being always annexed to the enjoyment of land, a submission to the government of the country, of which that land is a part; it has been commonly supposed, that a *father* could *oblige his posterity to that government*, of which he himself was a subject, and that his compact held them; whereas, it being only a necessary condition annexed to the land, and the inheritance of an estate which is under that government, reaches only those who will take it on that condition, and so is no natural tie or engagement, but a voluntary submission: for *every man's children* being by nature as *free* as himself, or any of his ancestors ever were, may, whilst they are in that freedom, choose what society they will join themselves to, what common-wealth they will put themselves under. But if they will enjoy the *inheritance* of their ancestors, they must take it on the same terms their ancestors had it, and submit to all the conditions annexed to such a possession. By this power indeed fathers oblige their children to obedience to themselves, even when they are past minority, and most commonly too subject them to this or that political power: but neither of these by any peculiar right of *fatherhood*, but by the reward they have in their hands to inforce and recompence such a compliance; and is no more power than what a *French man* has over an *English man*, who by the hopes of an estate he will leave him, will certainly have a strong tie on his obedience: and if, when it is left him, he will enjoy it, he must certainly take it upon the conditions annexed to the *possession of land* in that country where it lies, whether it be *France* or *England*.

§. 74. To conclude then, tho' the *father's power* of commanding extends no farther than the minority of his children, and to a degree only fit for the discipline and government of that age; and tho' that *honour* and *respect*, and all that which the *Latins* called *piety*, which they indispensibly owe to their parents all their life-time, and in all estates, with all that support and defence is due to them, gives the father no power of governing, *i. e.* making laws and enacting penalties on his children; though by all this he has no dominion over the property or actions of his son: yet it is obvious to conceive how easy it was, in the first ages of the world, and in places still, where the thinness of people gives families leave to separate into unpossessed quarters, and they have room to remove or plant themselves in yet vacant habitations, for the *father of the family* to become the prince of* it; he had been a ruler from the beginning of the infancy of his children: and since without some government it would be hard for them to live together, it was likeliest it should, by the express or tacit consent of the children when they were grown up, be in the father, where it seemed without any change barely to continue; when indeed nothing more was required to it, than the permitting the *father* to exercise alone, in his family, that executive power of the law of nature, which every free man naturally hath, and by that permission resigning up to him a monarchical power, whilst they remained in it. But that this was not by any *paternal right*, but only by the consent of his children, is evident from hence, that no body doubts, but if a stranger, whom chance or business had brought to his family, had there killed any of his children, or committed any other fact, he might condemn and put him to death, or otherwise have punished him, as well as any of his children; which it was impossible he should do by virtue of any paternal authority over one who was not his child, but by virtue of that executive power of the law of nature, which, as a man, he had a right to: and he alone could punish him in his family, where the respect of his children had laid by the exercise of such a power, to give way to the dignity and authority they were willing should remain in him, above the rest of his family.

§. 75. Thus it was easy, and almost natural for children, by a tacit, and scarce avoidable consent, to make way for the *father's authority and government*. They had been accustomed in their childhood to follow his direction, and to refer their little differences to him, and when they were men, who fitter to rule them? Their lit-

---

*It is no improbable opinion therefore, which the archphilosopher was of, that the chief person in every houshold was always, as it were, a king: so when numbers of housholds joined themselves in civil societies together, kings were the first kind of governors amongst them, which is also, as it seemeth, the reason why the name of fathers continued still in them, who, of fathers, were made rulers; as also the ancient custom of governors to do as *Melchizedec*, and being kings, to exercise the office of priests, which fathers did at the first, grew perhaps by the same occasion. Howbeit, this is not the only kind of regiment that has been received in the world. The inconveniences of one kind have caused sundry others to be devised; so that in a word, all public regiment, of what kind soever, seemeth evidently to have risen from the deliberate advice, consultation and composition between men, judging it convenient and behoveful; there being no impossibility in nature considered by itself, but that man might have lived without any public regiment, *Hooker's Eccl. P. lib.* i. *sect.* 10.

tle properties, and less covetousness, seldom afforded greater controversies; and when any should arise, where could they have a fitter umpire than he, by whose care they had every one been sustained and brought up, and who had a tenderness for them all? It is
no wonder that they made no distinction betwixt minority and full
age; nor looked after one and twenty, or any other age that might
make them the free disposers of themselves and fortunes, when they
could have no desire to be out of their pupilage: the government
they had been under, during it, continued still to be more their protection than restraint; and they could no where find a greater security to their peace, liberties, and fortunes, than in the *rule of a father.*

§. 76. Thus the natural *fathers of families*, by an insensible
change, became the *politic monarchs* of them too: and as they
chanced to live long, and leave able and worthy heirs, for several
successions, or otherwise; so they laid the foundations of
hereditary, or elective kingdoms, under several constitutions and
mannors, according as chance, contrivance, or occasions happened
to mould them. But if princes have their titles in their fathers right,
and it be a sufficient proof of the natural *right of fathers* to political
authority, because they commonly were those in whose hands we
find, *de facto,* the exercise of government: I say, if this argument be
good, it will as strongly prove, that all princes, nay princes only,
ought to be priests, since it is as certain, that in the beginning, *the
father of the family was priest, as that he was ruler in his own
houshold.*

CHAP. VII.

Of Political or Civil Society.

§. 77. GOD having made man such a creature, that in his own
judgment, it was not good for him to be alone, put him under strong
obligations of necessity, convenience, and inclination to drive him
into *society*, as well as fitted him with understanding and language
to continue and enjoy it. The *first society* was between man and
wife, which gave beginning to that between parents and children; to
which, in time, that between master and servant came to be added:
and though all these might, and commonly did meet together, and
make up but one family, wherein the master or mistress of it had
some sort of rule proper to a family; each of these, or all together,

came short of *political society*, as we shall see, if we consider the different ends, ties, and bounds of each of these.

§. 70. *Conjugal society* is made by a voluntary compact between man and woman; and tho' it consist chiefly in such a communion and right in one another's bodies as is necessary to its chief end, procreation; yet it draws with it mutual support and assistance, and a communion of interests too, as necessary not only to unite their care and affection, but also necessary to their common off-spring, who have a right to be nourished, and maintained by them, till they are able to provide for themselves.

§. 79. For the end of *conjunction, between male and female*, being not barely procreation, but the continuation of the species; this conjunction betwixt male and female ought to last, even after procreation, so long as is necessary to the nourishment and support of the young ones, who are to be sustained by those that got them, till they are able to shift and provide for themselves. This rule, which the infinite wise maker hath set to the works of his hands, we find the inferior creatures steadily obey. In those viviparous animals which feed on grass, the *conjunction between male and female* lasts no longer than the very act of copulation; because the teat of the dam being sufficient to nourish the young, till it be able to feed on grass, the male only begets, but concerns not himself for the female or young, to whose sustenance he can contribute nothing. But in beasts of prey the *conjunction* lasts longer: because the dam not being able well to subsist herself, and nourish her numerous off-spring by her own prey alone, a more laborious, as well as more dangerous way of living, than by feeding on grass, the assistance of the male is necessary to the maintenance of their common family, which cannot subsist till they are able to prey for themselves, but by the joint care of male and female. The same is to be observed in all birds, (except some domestic ones, where plenty of food excuses the cock from feeding, and taking care of the young brood) whose young needing food in the nest, the cock and hen continue mates, till the young are able to use their wing, and provide for themselves.

§. 80. And herein I think lies the chief, if not the only reason, *why the male and female in mankind are tied to a longer conjunction* than other creatures, *viz.* because the female is capable of conceiving, and *de facto* is commonly with child again, and brings forth too a new birth, long before the former is out of a dependency for support on his parents help, and able to shift for himself, and has all the assistance is due to him from his parents: whereby the father, who is bound to take care for those he hath begot, is under an obligation to continue in conjugal society with the same woman longer than other creatures, whose young being able to subsist of themselves, before the time of procreation returns again, the conjugal bond dissolves of itself, and they are at liberty, till *Hymen* at his usual anniversary season summons them again to chuse new mates. Wherein one cannot but admire the wisdom of the great Creator, who having given to man foresight, and an ability to lay up for the future, as well as to supply the present necessity, hath made it necessary, that *society of man and wife should be more lasting*, than of male and female amongst other creatures; that so their industry might be encouraged, and their interest better united, to make provision and lay up goods for their common issue, which uncertain mixture, or easy and frequent solutions of conjugal society would mightily disturb.

§. 81. But tho' these are ties upon *mankind*, which make the *conjugal bonds* more firm and lasting in man, than the other species of animals; yet it would give one reason to enquire, why this *compact*, where procreation and education are secured, and inheritance taken care for, may not be made determinable, either by consent, or at a certain time, or upon certain conditions, as well as any other voluntary compacts, there being no necessity in the nature of the thing, nor to the ends of it, that it should always be for life; I mean, to such as are under no restraint of any positive law, which ordains all such contracts to be perpetual.

§. 82. But the husband and wife, though they have but one common concern, yet having different understandings, will unavoidably sometimes have different wills too; it therefore being necessary that the last determination, *i. e.* the rule, should be placed somewhere; it naturally falls to the man's share, as the abler and the stronger. But this reaching but to the things of their common interest and property, leaves the wife in the full and free possession of what by contract is her peculiar right, and gives the husband no more power over her life than she has over his; the *power of the husband* being so far from that of an absolute monarch, that the *wife* has in many cases a liberty to separate from him, where natural right, or their contract allows it; whether that contract be made by themselves in the state of nature, or by the customs or laws of the country they live in; and the children upon such separation fall to the father or mother's lot, as such contract does determine.

§. 83. For all the ends of *marriage* being to be obtained under politic government, as well as in the state of nature, the civil magistrate doth not abridge the right or power of either naturally necessary to those ends, *viz.* procreation and mutual support and assistance whilst they are together; but only decides any controversy that may arise between man and wife about them. If it were otherwise, and that absolute *sovereignty* and power of life and death naturally belonged to the husband, and were *necessary to the society between man and wife.* there could be no matrimony in any of those countries where the husband is allowed no such absolute authority. But the ends of matrimony requiring no such power in the husband, the condition of *conjugal society* put it not in him, it being not at all necessary to that state. *Conjugal society* could subsist and attain its ends without it; nay, community of goods, and the power over them, mutual assistance and maintenance, and other things belonging to *conjugal society*, might be varied and regulated by that contract which unites man and wife in that society, as far as may consist with procreation and the bringing up of children till they could shift for themselves; nothing being necessary to any society, that is not necessary to the ends for which it is made.

§. 84. The *society betwixt parents and children*, and the distinct rights and powers belonging respectively to them, I have treated of so largely, in the foregoing chapter, that I shall not here need to say any thing of it. And I think it is plain, that it is far different from a politic society.

§. 85. *Master* and *servant* are names as old as history, but given to those of far different condition; for a freeman makes himself a servant to another, by selling him, for a certain time, the service he undertakes to do, in exchange for wages he is to receive: and though this commonly puts him into the family of his master, and under the ordinary discipline thereof; yet it gives the master but a temporary power over him, and no greater than what is contained in the *contract* between them. But there is another sort of servants, which by a peculiar name we call *slaves*, who being captives taken in a just war, are by the right of nature subjected to the absolute dominion and arbitrary power of their masters. These men having, as I say, forfeited their lives, and with it their liberties, and lost their estates; and being in the *state of slavery*, not capable of any property, cannot in that state be considered as any part of *civil society*; the chief end whereof is the preservation of property.

§. 86. Let us therefore consider a *master of a family* with all these subordinate relations of *wife, children, servants,* and *slaves,* united under the domestic rule of a family; which, what resemblance soever it may have in its order, offices, and number too, with a little common-wealth, yet is very far from it, both in its constitution, power and end: or if it must be thought a monarchy, and the *paterfamilias* the absolute monarch in it, absolute monarchy will have but a very shattered and short power, when it is plain, by what has been said before, that the *master of the family* has a very distinct and differently limited *power,* both as to time and extent, over those several persons that are in it; for excepting the slave (and the family is as much a family, and his power as *paterfamilias* as great, whether there be any slaves in his family or no) he has no legislative power of life and death over any of them, and none too but what a *mistress of a family* may have as well as he. And he certainly can have no absolute power over the whole *family,* who has but a very limited one over every individual in it. But how a *family,* or any other society of men, differ from that which is properly *political society,* we shall best see, by considering wherein *political society* itself consists.

§. 87. Man being born, as has been proved, with a title to perfect freedom, and an uncontrouled enjoyment of all the rights and privileges of the law of nature, equally with any other man, or number of men in the world, hath by nature a power, not only to preserve his property, that is, his life, liberty and estate, against the injuries and attempts of other men; but to judge of, and punish the breaches of that law in others, as he is persuaded the offence deserves, even with death itself, in crimes where the heinousness of the fact, in his opinion, requires it. But because no *political society* can be, nor subsist, without having in itself the power to preserve the property, and in order thereunto, punish the offences of all those of that society; there, and there only is *political society,* where every one of the members hath quitted this natural power, resigned it up into the hands of the community in all cases that exclude him not from appealing for protection to the law established by it. And thus all private judgment of every particular member being excluded, the community comes to be umpire, by settled standing rules, indifferent, and the same to all parties; and by men having authority from the community, for the execution of those rules, decides all the differences that may happen between any members of that society concerning any matter of right; and punishes those offences which any member hath committed against the society, with such penalties as the law has established: whereby it is easy to discern, who are, and who are not, in *political society* together. Those who are united into one body, and have a common established law and judicature to appeal to, with authority to decide controversies between them, and punish offenders, are in *civil society* one with another: but those who have no such common appeal, I mean on earth, are still in the state of nature, each being, where there is no other, judge for himself, and executioner; which is, as I have before shewed it, the perfect *state of nature*.

§. 88. And thus the common-wealth comes by a power to set down what punishment shall belong to the several transgressions which they think worthy of it, committed amongst the members of that society, (which is the *power of making laws)* as well as it has the power to punish any injury done unto any of its members, by any one that is not of it, (which is the *power of war and peace;)* and all this for the preservation of the property of all the members of that society, as far as is possible. But though every man who has entered into civil society, and is become a member of any common-wealth, has thereby quitted his power to punish offences, against the law of *nature,* in prosecution of his own private judgment, yet with the judgment of offences, which he has given up to the legislative in all cases, where he can appeal to the magistrate, he has given a right to the common-wealth to employ his force, for the execution of the judgments of the common-wealth, whenever he shall be called to it; which indeed are his own judgments, they being made by himself, or his representative. And herein we have the original of the *legislative* and *executive power* of civil society, which is to judge by standing laws, how far offences are to be punished, when committed within the common-wealth; and also to determine, by occasional judgments founded on the present circumstances of the fact, how far injuries from without are to be vindicated; and in both these to employ all the force of all the members, when there shall be need.

§. 89. Where-ever therefore any number of men are so united into one society, as to quit every one his executive power of the law of nature, and to resign it to the public, there and there only is a *political, or civil society.* And this is done, where-ever any number of men, in the state of nature, enter into society to make one people, one body politic, under one supreme government; or else when any one joins himself to, and incorporates with any government already made: for hereby he authorizes the society, or which is all one, the legislative thereof, to make laws for him, as the public good of the society shall require; to the execution whereof, his own assistance (as to his own decrees) is due. And this *puts men* out of a state of nature *into* that of a *common-wealth*, by setting up a judge on earth, with authority to determine all the controversies, and redress the injuries that may happen to any member of the common-wealth; which judge is the legislative, or magistrates appointed by it. And where-ever there are any number of men, however associated, that have no such decisive power to appeal to, there they are still in *the state of nature.*

§. 90. Hence it is evident, that *absolute monarchy*, which by some men is counted the only government in the world, is indeed *inconsistent with civil society*, and so can be no form of civil-government at all: for the *end of civil society*, being to avoid, and remedy those inconveniencies of the state of nature, which necessarily follow from every man's being judge in his own case, by setting up a known authority, to which every one of that society may appeal upon any injury received, or controversy that may arise, and which every one of the* society ought to obey; where-ever any persons are, who have not such an authority to appeal to, for the decision of any difference between them, there those persons are still *in the state of nature*; and so is every *absolute prince*, in respect of those who are under his *dominion.*

§. 91. For he being supposed to have all, both legislative and executive power in himself alone, there is no judge to be found, no appeal lies open to any one, who may fairly, and indifferently, and with authority decide, and from whose decision relief and redress may be expected of any injury or inconviency, that may be suffered from the prince, or by his order: so that such a man, however intitled, *Czar*, or *Grand Seignior*, or how you please, is as much *in the state of nature*, with all under his dominion, as he is with the

*The public power of all society is above every soul contained in the same society; and the principal use of that power is, to give laws unto all that are under it, which laws in such cases we must obey, unless there be reason shewed which may necessarily inforce, that the law of reason, or of God, doth enjoin the contrary, *Hook. Eccl. Pol. l. i. sect.* 16.

rest of mankind: for where-ever any two men are, who have no standing rule, and common judge to appeal to on earth, for the determination of controversies of right betwixt them, there they are still *in the state of* nature,* and under all the inconveniencies of it, with only this woful difference to the subject, or rather slave of an absolute prince: that whereas, in the ordinary state of nature, he has a liberty to judge of his right, and according to the best of his power, to maintain it; now, whenever his property is invaded by the will and order of his monarch, he has not only no appeal, as those in society ought to have, but as if he were degraded from the common state of rational creatures, is denied a liberty to judge of, or to defend his right; and so is exposed to all the misery and inconveniencies, that a man can fear from one, who being in the unrestrained state of nature, is yet corrupted with flattery, and armed with power.

§. 92. For he that thinks *absolute power purifies men's blood,* and corrects the baseness of human nature, need read but the history of this, or any other age, to be convinced of the contrary. He that would have been insolent and injurious in the woods of *America,* would not probably be much better in a throne; where perhaps learning and religion shall be found out to justify all that he shall do to his subjects, and the sword presently silence all those that dare question it: for what the *protection of absolute monarchy* is, what kind of fathers of their countries it makes princes to be and to what a degree of happiness and security it carries civil society, where this sort of government is grown to perfection, he that will look into the late relation of *Ceylon,* may easily

---

*To take away all such mutual grievances, injuries and wrongs, *i. e.* such as at tend men in the state of nature, there was no way but only by growing into composition and agreement amongst themselves, by ordaining some kind of government public, and by yielding themselves subject thereunto, that unto whom they granted authority to rule and govern, by them the peace, tranquillity and happy estate of the rest might be procured. Men always knew that where force and injury was offered, they might be defenders of themselves; they knew that however men may seek their own commodity, yet if this were done with injury unto others, it was not to be suffered, but by all men, and all good means to be withstood. Finally, they knew that no man might in reason take upon him to determine his own right, and according to his own determination proceed in maintenance thereof, in as much as every man is towards himself, and them whom he greatly affects, partial; and therefore that strifes and troubles would be endless, except they gave their common consent, all to be ordered by some, whom they should agree upon, without which consent there would be no reason that one man should take upon him to be lord or judge over another, *Hooker's Eccl. Pol. l.* i. *sect.* 10.

see.

§. 93. In *absolute monarchies* indeed, as well as other governments of the world, the subjects have an appeal to the law, and
judges to decide any controversies, and restrain any violence that
may happen betwixt the subjects themselves, one amongst another.
This every one thinks necessary, and believes he deserves to be
thought a declared enemy to society and mankind, who should go
about to take it away. But whether this be from a true love of
mankind and society, and such a charity as we owe all one to
another, there is reason to doubt: for this is no more than what
every man, who loves his own power, profit, or greatness, may and
naturally must do, keep those animals from hurting, or destroying one another, who labour and drudge only for his pleasure
and advantage; and so are taken care of, not out of any love the
master has for them, but love of himself, and the profit they bring
him: for if it be asked, what security, *what fence* is there, in
such a state, *against the violence and oppression of this absolute
ruler?* the very question can scarce be borne. They are ready to tell
you, that it deserves death only to ask after safety. Betwixt subject
and subject, they will grant, there must be measures, laws and
judges, for their mutual peace and security: but as for the *ruler,*
he ought to be *absolute,* and is above all such circumstances;
because he has power to do more hurt and wrong, it is right when
he does it. To ask how you may be guarded from harm, or injury,
on that side where the strongest hand is to do it, is presently the
voice of faction and rebellion: as if when men quitting the state of
nature entered into society, they agreed that all of them but one,
should be under the restraint of laws, but that he should still retain
all the liberty of the state of nature, increased with power, and
made licentious by impunity. This is to think, that men are so
foolish, that they take care to avoid what mischiefs may be done
them by *pole-cats,* or *foxes;* but are content, nay, think it safety, to
be devoured by *lions.*

§. 94. But whatever flatterers may talk to amuse people's
understandings, it hinders not men from feeling; and when they
perceive, that any man, in what station soever, is out of the bounds
of the civil society which they are of, and that they have no appeal
on earth against any harm, they may receive from him, they are apt
to think themselves in the state of nature, in respect of him whom
they find to be so; and to take care, as soon as they can, to have
that *safety and security in civil society,* for which it was first

instituted, and for which only they entered into it. And therefore, though perhaps at first , (as shall be shewed more at large hereafter in the following part of this discourse) some one good and excellent man having got a pre-eminency amongst the rest, had this deference paid to his goodness and virtue, as to a kind of natural authority, that the chief rule, with arbitration of their differences, by a tacit consent devolved into his hands, without any other caution, but the assurance they had of his uprightness and wisdom; yet when time, giving authority, and (as some men would persuade us) sacredness of customs, which the negligent, and unforeseeing innocence of the first ages began, had brought in successors of another stamp, the people finding their properties not secure under the government, as then it was, (whereas government has no other end but the preservation of* property) could never be safe nor at rest, *nor think themselves in civil society,* till the legislature was placed in collective bodies of men, call them senate, parliament, or what you please. By which means every single person became subject, equally with other the meanest men, to those laws, which he himself, as part of the legislative, had established; nor could any one, by his own authority; avoid the force of the law, when once made; nor by any pretence of superiority plead exemption, thereby to license his own, or the miscarriages of any of his dependents.†
No man in civil society can be exempted from the laws of it: for if any man may do what he thinks fit, and there be no appeal on earth, for redress or security against any harm he shall do; I ask, whether he be not perfectly still in the state of nature, and so can be *no part or member of that civil society;* unless any one will say, the state of nature and civil society are one and the same thing, which I have never yet found any one so great a patron of anarchy as to affirm.

---

*At the first, when some certain kind of regiment was once appointed, it may be that nothing was then farther thought upon for the manner of governing, but all permitted unto their wisdom and discretion, which were to rule, till by experience they found this for all parts very inconvenient, so as the thing which they had devised for a remedy, did indeed but increase the sore, which it should have cured. They saw, that *to live by one man's will, became the cause of all men's misery.* This constrained them to come unto laws, wherein all men might see their duty beforehand, and know the penalties of transgressing them. *Hooker's Eccl. Pol. l.* i. *sect.* 10.

†Civil law being the act of the whole body politic, doth therefore over-rule each several part of the same body. *Hooker, ibid.*

CHAP. VIII.

Of the Beginning of Political Societies.

§. 95. MEN being, as has been said, by nature, all free, equal, and independent, no one can be put out of this estate, and subjected to the political power of another, without his own consent. The only way whereby any one divests himself of his natural liberty, and puts on the *bonds of civil society,* is by agreeing with other men to join and unite into a community for their comfortable, safe, and peaceable living one amongst another, in a secure enjoyment of their properties, and a greater security against any, that are not of it. This any number of men may do, because it injures not the freedom of the rest; they are left as they were in the liberty of the state of nature. When any number of men have so *consented to make one community or government,* they are thereby presently incorporated, and make *one body politic,* wherein the *majority* have a right to act and conclude the rest.

§. 96. For when any number of men have, by the consent of every individual, made a *community,* they have thereby made that *community* one body, with a power to act as one body, which is only by the will and determination of the *majority:* for that which acts any community, being only the consent of the individuals of it, and it being necessary to that which is one body to move one way; it is necessary the body should move that way whither the greater force carries it, which is the *consent of the majority:* or else it is impossible it should act or continue one body, *one community,* which the consent of every individual that united into it, agreed that it should; and so every one is bound by that consent to be concluded by the *majority.* And therefore we see, that in assemblies, impowered to act by positive laws, where no number is set by that positive law which impowers them, the *act of the majority* passes for the act of the whole, and of course determines, as having, by the law of nature and reason, the power of the whole.

§. 97. And thus every man, by consenting with others to make one body politic under one government, puts himself under an obligation, to every one of that society, to submit to the determination of the *majority,* and to be concluded by it; or else this *original compact,* whereby he with others incorporates into *one society,* would signify nothing, and be no compact, if he be left free, and under no other ties than he was in before in the state of nature. For what appearance would there be of any compact? what new engagement if he were no farther tied by any decrees of the society, than he himself thought fit, and did actually consent to? This would be still as great a liberty, as he himself had before his compact, or any one else in the state of nature hath, who may submit himself, and consent to any acts of it if he thinks fit.

§. 98. For if *the consent of the majority* shall not, in reason, be received as *the act of the whole,* and conclude every individual; nothing but the consent of every individual can make any thing to be the act of the whole: but such a consent is next to impossible ever to be had, if we consider the infirmities of health, and avocations of business, which in a number, though much less than that of a common-wealth, will necessarily keep many away from the public assembly. To which if we add the variety of opinions, and contrariety of interests, which unavoidably happen in all collections of men, the coming into society upon such terms would be only like *Cato's* coming into the theatre, only to go out again. Such a constitution as this would make the mighty *Leviathan* of a shorter duration, than the feeblest creatures, and not let it outlast the day it was born in: which cannot be supposed, till we can think, that rational creatures should desire and constitute societies only to be dissolved: for where the *majority* cannot conclude the rest, there they cannot act as one body, and consequently will be immediately dissolved again.

§. 99. Whosoever therefore out of a state of nature unite into a *community,* must be understood to give up all the power, necessary to the ends for which they unite into society, to the *majority* of the community, unless they expresly agreed in any number greater than the majority. And this is done by barely agreeing to *unite into one political society,* which is *all the compact* that is, or needs be, between the individuals, that enter into, or make up a *common-wealth.* And thus that, which begins and actually *constitutes any political society,* is nothing but the consent of any number of freemen capable of a majority to unite and incorporate into such a society. And this is that, and that only, which did, or could give beginning to any *lawful government* in the world.

§. 100. To this I find two objections made.

First, *That there are no instances to be found in story, of a company of men independent, and equal one amongst another, that met together, and in this way began and set up a government.*

Secondly, *It is impossible of right, that men should do so,*
because all men being born under government, they are to submit to
that, and are not at liberty to begin a new one.

§. 101. To the first there is this to answer, That it is not at all to
be wondered, that *history* gives us but a very little account of *men,*
that lived together in the state of nature. The inconveniences of that
condition, and the love and want of society, no sooner brought any
number of them together, but they presently united and incorporated, if they designed to continue together. And if we may not
suppose *men* ever to have been *in the state of nature*, because we
hear not much of them in such a state, we may as well suppose the
armies of *Salmanasser* or *Xerxes* were never children, because we
hear little of them, till they were men, and imbodied in armies.
Government is every where antecedent to records, and letters
seldom come in amongst a people till a long continuation of civil
society has, by other more necessary arts, provided for their safety,
ease, and plenty: and then they begin to look after the history of
their founders, and search into their *original*, when they have
outlived the memory of it: for it is with *common-wealths* as with
particular persons, they are commonly *ignorant of their own births*
and infancies: and if they know any thing of their *original*, they are
beholden for it, to the accidental records that others have kept of it.
And those that we have, of the beginning of any polities in the
world, excepting that of the *Jews*, where God himself immediately
interposed, and which favours not at all paternal dominion, are all
either plain instances of such a beginning as I have mentioned, or at
least have manifest footsteps of it.

§. 102. He must shew a strange inclination to deny evident matter of fact, when it agrees not with his hypothesis, who will not
allow, that the *beginning* of *Rome* and *Venice* were by the uniting
together of several men free and independent one of another,
amongst whom there was no natural superiority or subjection. And
if *Josephus Acosta's* word may be taken, he tells us, that in many
parts of *America* there was no government at all. *There are great*
and apparent conjectures, says he, *that these men*, speaking of those
of Peru, *for a long time had neither kings nor common-wealths, but*
lived in troops, as they do this day in Florida, *the* Cheriquanas,
those of Brazil, *and many other nations, which have no certain*
kings, but as occasion is offered, in peace or war, they choose their
captains as they please, l. i. c. 25. If it be said, that every man there
was born subject to his father, or the head of his family; that the

subjection due from a child to a father took not away his freedom of uniting into what political society he thought fit, has been already proved. But be that as it will, these men, it is evident, were actually *free;* and whatever superiority some politicians now would place in any of them, they themselves claimed it not, but by consent were all *equal,* till by the same consent they set rulers over themselves. So that their *politic societies* all *began* from a voluntary union, and the mutual agreement of men freely acting in the choice of their governors, and forms of government.

§. 103. And I hope those who went away from *Sparta* with *Palantus,* mentioned by *Justin,* l. iii. c. 4. will be allowed to have been *freemen independent* one of another, and to have set up a government over themselves, by their own consent. Thus I have given several examples, out of history, of *people free and in the state of nature,* that being met together incorporated and *began a common-wealth.* And if the want of such instances be an argument to prove that *government* were not, nor could not be so *begun,* I suppose the contenders for paternal empire were better let it alone, than urge it against natural liberty: for if they can give so many instances, out of history, of *governments begun* upon paternal right, I think (though at best an argument from what has been, to what should of right be, has no great force) one might, without any great danger, yield them the cause. But if I might advise them in the case, they would do well not to search too much into the *original of governments,* as they have begun *de facto,* lest they should find, at the foundation of most of them, something very little favourable to the design they promote, and such a power as they contend for.

§. 104. But to conclude, reason being plain on our side, that men are naturally free, and the examples of history shewing, that the *governments* of the world, that were begun in peace, had their beginning laid on that foundation, and were *made by the consent of the people;* there can be little room for doubt, either where the right is, or what has been the opinion, or practice of mankind, about the *first erecting of governments.*

§. 105. I will not deny, that if we look back as far as history will direct us, towards the *original of common-wealths,* we shall generally find them under the government and administration of one man. And I am also apt to believe, that where a family was numerous enough to subsist by itself, and continued entire together, without mixing with others, as it often happens, where there is much land, and few people, the government commonly began in the father: for the father having, by the law of nature, the same power with every man else to punish, as he thought fit, any offences against that law, might thereby punish his transgressing children, even when they were men, and out of their pupilage; and they were very likely to submit to his punishment, and all join with him against the offender, in their turns, giving him thereby power to execute his sentence against any transgression, and so in effect make him the law-maker, and governor over all that remained in conjunction with his family. He was fittest to be trusted; paternal affection secured their property and interest under his care; and the custom of obeying him, in their childhood, made it easier to submit to him, rather than to any other. If therefore they must have one to rule them, as government is hardly to be avoided amongst men that live together; who so likely to be the man as he that was their common father; unless negligence, cruelty, or any other defect of mind or body made him unfit for it? But when either the father died, and left his next heir, for want of age, wisdom, courage, or any other qualities, less fit for rule; or where several families met, and consented to continue together; there, it is not to be doubted, but they used their natural freedom, to set up him, whom they judged the ablest, and most likely, to rule well over them. Conformable hereunto we find the people of *America*, who (living out of the reach of the conquering swords, and spreading domination of the two great empires of *Peru* and *Mexico*) enjoyed their own natural freedom, though, *caeteris paribus*, they commonly prefer the heir of their deceased king; yet if they find him any way weak, or uncapable, they pass him by, and set up the stoutest and bravest man for their ruler.

§. 106. Thus, though looking back as far as records give us any account of peopling the world, and the history of nations, we commonly find the *government* to be in one hand; yet it destroys not that which I affirm, *viz.* that the *beginning of politic society* depends upon the consent of the individuals, to join into, and make one society; who, when they are thus incorporated, might set up what form of government they thought fit. But this having given occasion to men to mistake, and think, that by nature government was monarchical, and belonged to the father, it may not be amiss here to consider, why people in the beginning generally pitched upon this form, which though perhaps the father's pre-eminence might, in the first institution of some common-wealths, give a rise to, and place in the beginning, the power in one hand; yet it is plain that the reason, that continued the form of *government in a single person*, was not any regard, or respect to paternal authority: since all petty *monarchies*, that is, almost all monarchies, near their original, have been commonly, at least upon occasion, *elective*.

§. 107. First then, in the beginning of things, the father's government of the childhood of those sprung from him, having accustomed them to the *rule of one man*, and taught them that where it was exercised with care and skill, with affection and love to those under it, it was sufficient to procure and preserve to men all the political happiness they sought for in society. It was no wonder that they should pitch upon, and naturally run into that form of government, which from their infancy they had been all accustomed to; and which, by experience, they had found both easy and safe. To which, if we add, that *monarchy* being simple, and most obvious to men, whom neither experience had instructed in forms of government, nor the ambition or insolence of empire had taught to beware of the encroachments of prerogative, or the inconveniences of absolute power, which monarchy in succession was apt to lay claim to, and bring upon them, it was not at all strange, that they should not much trouble themselves to think of methods of restraining any exorbitances of those to whom they had given the authority over them, and of balancing the power of government, by placing several parts of it in different hands. They had neither felt the oppression of tyrannical dominion, nor did the fashion of the age, nor their possessions, or way of living, (which afforded little matter for covetousness or ambition) give them any reason to apprehend or provide against it; and therefore it is no wonder they put themselves into such a *frame of government*, as was not only, as I said, most obvious and simple, but also best suited to their present state and condition; which stood more in need of defence against foreign invasions and injuries, than of multiplicity of laws. The equality of a simple poor way of living, confining their desires within the narrow bounds of each man's small property, made few controversies, and so no need of many laws to decide them, or variety of officers to superintend the process, or look after the execution of justice, where there were but few trespasses, and few offenders. Since then those, who like one another so well as to join into society, cannot but be supposed to have some acquaintance and friendship together, and some trust one in another; they could not but have greater apprehensions of others, than of one another: and therefore their first care and thought cannot but be supposed to be, how to secure themselves against foreign force. It was natural for them to put themselves under a *frame of government* which might best serve to that end, and chuse the wisest and bravest man to conduct them in their wars, and lead them out against their enemies, and in this chiefly be their *ruler*.

§. 108. Thus we see, that the *kings* of the *Indians* in *America*, which is still a pattern of the first ages in *Asia* and *Europe*, whilst the inhabitants were too few for the country, and want of people and money gave men no temptation to enlarge their possessions of land, or contest for wider extent of ground, are little more than *generals of their armies;* and though they command absolutely in war, yet at home and in time of peace they exercise very little dominion, and have but a very moderate sovereignty, the resolutions of peace and war being ordinarily either in the people, or in a council. Tho' the war itself, which admits not of plurality of governors, naturally devolves the command into the *king's sole authority*.

§. 109. And thus in *Israel* itself, the *chief business of their judges, and first kings,* seems to have been *to be captains in war,* and leaders of their armies; which (besides what is signified by *going out and in before the people,* which was, to march forth to war, and home again in the heads of their forces) appears plainly in the story of *Jephtha*. The *Ammonites* making war upon *Israel,* the *Gileadites* in fear send to *Jephtha,* a bastard of their family whom they had cast off, and article with him, if he will assist them against the *Ammonites,* to make him their ruler; which they do in these words, *And the people made him head and captain over them,* Judg. xi, 11. which was, as it seems, all one as to be *judge. And he judged Israel,* Judg. xii. 7. that is, was their *captain-general six years*. So when *Jotham* upbraids the *Shechemites* with the obligation they had to *Gideon,* who had been their *judge* and ruler, he tells them, *He fought for you, and adventured his life far, and delivered you out of the hands of Midian,* Judg. ix. 17. Nothing mentioned of him but what he did as a *general:* and indeed that is all is found in his history, or in any of the rest of the judges. And *Abimelech* particularly is called *king,* though at most he was but their *general.* And when, being weary of the ill conduct of *Samuel's* sons, the children of *Israel* desired a *king, like all the nations to judge them, and to go out before them, and to fight their battles,* I. Sam viii. 20. God granting their desire, says to *Samuel, I will send thee a man, and thou shalt anoint him to be captain over my people Israel, that he may save my people out of the hands of the Philistines,* ix. 16. As if the only *business of a king* had been to lead out their armies, and fight in their defence; and accordingly at his inauguration pouring a vial of oil upon him, declares to Saul, that *the Lord had anointed him to be captain over his inheritance*, x. 1. And therefore those, who after *Saul's* being solemnly chosen and saluted *king* by the *tribes* at *Mispah*, were unwilling to have him their king, made no other objection but this, *How shall this man save us?* v. 27. as if they should have said, this man is unfit to be our *king*, not having skill and conduct enough in war, to be able to defend us. And when God resolved to transfer the government to *David*, it is in these words, *But now thy kingdom shall not continue: the Lord hath sought him a man after his own heart, and the Lord hath commanded him to be captain over his people*, xiii. 14. As if the whole *kingly authority* were nothing else but to be their *general:* and therefore the *tribes* who had stuck to *Saul's* family, and opposed *David's* reign, when they came to *Hebron* with terms of submission to him, they tell him, amongst other arguments they had to submit to him as to their king, that he was in effect their *king* in *Saul's* time, and therefore they had no reason but to receive him as their *king* now. *Also* (say they) *in time past, when Saul was king over us, thou wast he that leddest out and broughtest in Israel, and the Lord said unto thee, Thou shalt feed my people Israel, and thou shalt be a captain over Israel.*

§. 110. Thus, whether *a family* by degrees *grew up into a common-wealth*, and the fatherly authority being continued on to the elder son, every one in his turn growing up under it, tacitly submitted to it, and the easiness and equality of it not offending any one, every one acquiesced, till time seemed to have confirmed it, and settled a right of succession by prescription: or whether several families, or the descendants of several families, whom chance, neighbourhood, or business brought together, uniting into society, the need of a general, whose conduct might defend them against their enemies in war, and the great confidence the innocence and sincerity of that poor but virtuous age, (such as are almost all those which begin governments, that ever come to last in the world) gave men one of another, made the first beginners of common-wealths generally put the rule into one man's hand, without any other express limitation or restraint, but what the nature of the thing, and the end of government required: which ever of those it was that at first put the rule into the hands of a single person, certain it is no body was intrusted with it but for the public good and safety, and to those ends, in the infancies of common-wealths, those who had it commonly used it. And unless they had done so, young societies could not have subsisted; without such nursing fathers tender and careful of the public weal, all governments would have sunk under the weakness and infirmities of their infancy, and the prince and the people had soon perished together.

§. 111. But though the *golden age* (before vain ambition, and *amor sceleratus habendi*, evil concupiscence, had corrupted men's minds into a mistake of true power and honour) had more virtue, and consequently better governors, as well as less vicious subjects, and there was then *no stretching prerogative* on the one side, to oppress the people; *nor* consequently on the other, any *dispute about privilege*, to lessen or restrain the power of the magistrate, and so no contest betwixt rulers and people about governors or government: yet, when ambition and luxury in future ages* would retain and increase the power, without doing the business for which it was given; and aided by flattery, taught princes to have distinct and separate interests from their people, men found it necessary to examine more carefully *the original* and rights *of government;* and to find out ways to *restrain the exorbitances,* and *prevent the abuses* of that power, which they having intrusted in another's hands only for their own good, they found was made use of to hurt them.

§. 112. Thus we may see how probable it is, that people that were naturally free, and by their own consent either submitted to the government of their father, or united together out of different families to make a government, should generally put the *rule into one man's hands,* and chuse to be under the conduct of a *single person,* without so much as by express conditions limiting or regulating his power, which they thought safe enough in his honesty and prudence; though they never dreamed of monarchy being *Jure Divino,* which we never heard of among mankind, till it was revealed to us by the divinity of this last age; nor ever allowed paternal power to have a right to dominion, or to be the foundation of all

---

*At first, when some certain kind of regiment was once approved, it may be nothing was then farther thought upon for the manner of governing, but all permitted unto their wisdom and discretion which were to rule, till by experience they found this for all parts very inconvenient, so as the thing which they had devised for a remedy, did indeed but increase the sore which it should have cured. They saw, that to live by one man's will, became the cause of all men's misery. This constrained them to come unto laws wherein all men might see their duty before hand, and know the penalties of transgressing them. *Hooker's Eccl. Pol. l. i. sect. 10.*

government. And thus much may suffice to shew, that as far as we have any light from history, we have reason to conclude, that all peaceful beginnings of *government* have been *laid in the consent of the people.* I say *peaceful,* because I shall have occasion in another place to speak of conquest, which some esteem a way of beginning of governments.

The other objection I find urged against the beginning of polities, in the way I have mentioned, is this, viz.

§. 113. *That all men being born under government, some or other, it is impossible any of them should ever be free, and at liberty to unite together, and begin a new one, or ever be able to erect a lawful government.*

If this argument be good; I ask, how came so many lawful monarchies into the world? for if any body, upon this supposition, can shew me any one man in any age of the world *free* to begin a lawful monarchy, I will be bound to shew him ten other *free men* at liberty, at the same time to unite and begin a new government under a regal, or any other form; it being demonstration, that if any one, *born under the dominion* of another, may be so *free* as to have a right to command others in a new and distinct empire, every one that is *born under the dominion* of another may be so free too, and may become a ruler, or subject, of a distinct separate government. And so by this their own principle, either all men, however *born,* are *free,* or else there is but one lawful prince, one lawful government in the world. And then they have nothing to do, but barely to shew us which that is; which when they have done, I doubt not but all mankind will easily agree to pay obedience to him.

§. 114. Though it be a sufficient answer to their objection, to shew that it involves them in the same difficulties that it doth those they use it against; yet I shall endeavour to discover the weakness of this argument a little farther.

All men, say they, *are born under government, and therefore they cannot be at liberty to begin a new one. Every one is born a subject to his father, or his prince, and is therefore under the perpetual tie of subjection and allegiance.* It is plain mankind never owned nor considered any such natural *subjection that they were born in,* to one or to the other that tied them, without their own consents, to a subjection to them and their heirs.

§. 115. For there are no examples so frequent in history, both sacred and profane, as those of men withdrawing themselves, and their obedience, from the jurisdiction they were born under, and the family or community they were bred up in, and *setting up new governments* in other places; from whence sprang all that number of petty common-wealths in the beginning of ages, and which always multiplied, as long as there was room enough, till the stronger, or more fortunate, swallowed the weaker; and those great ones again breaking to pieces, dissolved into lesser dominions. All which are so many testimonies against paternal sovereignty, and plainly prove, that it was not the natural right of the *father* descending to his heirs, that made governments in the beginning, since it was impossible, upon that ground, there should have been so many little kingdoms; all must have been but only one universal monarchy, if men had not been at *liberty to separate* themselves from their families, and the government, be it what it will, that was set up in it, and go and make distinct common-wealths and other governments, as they thought fit.

§. 116. This has been the practice of the world from its first beginning to this day; nor is it now any more hindrance to the freedom of mankind, that they are *born under constituted and ancient polities,* that have established laws, and set forms of government, than if they were born in the woods, amongst the unconfined inhabitants, that run loose in them: for those, who would persuade us, that *by being born under any government, we are naturally subjects to it,* and have no more any title or pretence to the freedom of the state of nature, have no other reason (bating that of paternal power, which we have already answered) to produce for it, but only, because our fathers or progenitors passed away their natural liberty, and thereby bound up themselves and their posterity to a perpetual subjection to the government, which they themselves submitted to. It is true, that whatever engagements or promises any one has made for himself, he is under the obligation of them, but *cannot,* by any *compact* whatsoever, *bind his children or posterity:* for his son, when a man, being altogether as free as the father, any *act of the father can no more give away the liberty of the son,* than it can of any body else: he may indeed annex such conditions to the land, he enjoyed as a subject of any common-wealth, as may oblige his son to be of that community, if he will enjoy those possessions which were his father's; because that estate being his father's property, he may dispose, or settle it, as he pleases.

§. 117. And this has generally given the occasion to mistake in this matter; because common-wealths not permitting any part of their dominions to be dismembered, nor to be enjoyed by any but those of their community, the son cannot ordinarily enjoy the possessions of his father, but under the same terms his father did, by becoming a member of the society; whereby he puts himself presently under the government he finds there established, as much as any other subject of that common-wealth. And thus *the consent of freemen, born under government,* which only *makes them members of it,* being given separately in their turns, as each comes to be of age, and not in a multitude together; people take no notice of it, and thinking it not done at all, or not necessary, conclude they are naturally subjects as they are men.

§. 118. But, it is plain, *governments* themselves understand it otherwise; they claim *no power over the son, because of that they had over the father;* nor look on children as being their subjects, by their fathers being so. If a subject of *England* have a child, by an *English* woman in *France,* whose subject is he? Not the king of *England*'s; for he must have leave to be admitted to the privileges of it: nor the king of *France*'s; for how then has his father a liberty to bring him away, and breed him as he pleases? and who ever was judged as a *traytor* or *deserter,* if he left, or warred against a country, for being barely born in it of parents that were aliens there? It is plain then, by the practice of governments themselves, as well as by the law of right reason, that *a child is born a subject of no country or government.* He is under his father's tuition and authority, till he comes to age of discretion; and then he is a freeman, at liberty what government he will put himself under, what body politic he will unite himself to: for if an *Englishman*'s son, born in *France,* be at liberty, and may do so, it is evident there is no tie upon him by his father's being a subject of this kingdom; nor is he bound up by any compact of his ancestors. And why then hath not his son, by the same reason, the same liberty, though he be born any where else? Since the power that a father hath naturally over his children, is the same, where-ever they be born, and the ties of natural obligations, are not bounded by the positive limits of kingdoms and common-wealths.

§. 119. *Every man* being, as has been shewed, *naturally free,* and nothing being able to put him into subjection to any earthly power, but only his own *consent;* it is to be considered, what shall be understood to be a *sufficient declaration* of a man's *consent, to make him subject* to the laws of any government. There is a common distinction of an express and a tacit consent, which will concern our present case. No body doubts but an express *consent,* of any man entering into any society, makes him a perfect member of that society, a subject of that government. The difficulty is, what ought to be looked upon as a *tacit consent*, and how far it binds, *i.e.* how far any one shall be looked on to have consented, and thereby submitted to any government, where he has made no expressions of it at all. And to this I say, that every man, that hath any possessions, or enjoyment, of any part of the dominions of any government, doth thereby give his *tacit consent*, and is as far forth obliged to obedience to the laws of that government, during such enjoyment, as any one under it; whether this his possession be of land, to him and his heirs for ever, or a lodging only for a week; or whether it be barely travelling freely on the highway; and in effect, it reaches as far as the very being of any one within the territories of that government.

§. 120. To understand this the better, it is fit to consider, that every man, when he at first incorporates himself into any commonwealth, he, by his uniting himself thereunto, annexed also, and submits to the community, those possessions, which he has, or shall acquire, that do not already belong to any other government: for it would be a direct contradiction, for any one to enter into society with others for the securing and regulating of property; and yet to suppose his land, whose property is to be regulated by the laws of the society, should be exempt from the jurisdiction of that government, to which he himself, the proprietor of the land, is a subject. By the same act therefore, whereby any one unites his person, which was before free, to any common-wealth, by the same he unites his possessions, which were before free, to it also; and they become, both of them, person and possession, subject to the government and dominion of that common-wealth, as long as it hath a being. Whoever therefore, from thenceforth, by inheritance, purchase, permission, or otherways, *enjoys any part of the land*, so annexed to, and under the government *of that common-wealth, must take it with the condition* it is under; that is, *of submitting to the government of the common-wealth*, under whose jurisdiction it is, as far forth as any subject of it.

§. 121. But since the government has a direct jurisdiction only over the land, and reaches the possessor of it, (before he has actually incorporated himself in the society) only as he dwells upon, and enjoys that; the obligation any one is under, by virtue of such enjoyment, to *submit to the government, begins and ends with the enjoyment*; so that whenever the owner, who has given nothing but such a *tacit consent* to the government, will, by donation, sale, or otherwise, quit the said possession, he is at liberty to go and incorporate himself into any other common-wealth; or to agree with others to begin a new one, *in vacuis locis*, in any part of the world, they can find free and unpossessed: whereas he, that has once, by actual agreement, and any *express* declaration, given his *consent* to be of any common-wealth, is perpetually and indispensibly obliged to be, and remain unalterably a subject to it, and can never be again in the liberty of the state of nature; unless, by any calamity, the government he was under comes to be dissolved; or else by some public act cuts him off from being any longer a member of it.

§. 122. But submitting to the laws of any country, living quietly, and enjoying privileges and protection under them, *makes not a man a member of that society:* this is only a local protection and homage due to and from all those, who, not being in a state of war, come within the territories belonging to any government, to all parts whereof the force of its laws extends. But this no more *makes a man a member of that society*, a perpetual subject of that common-wealth, than it would make a man a subject to another, in whose family he found it convenient to abide for some time; though, whilst he continued in it, he were obliged to comply with the laws, and submit to the government he found there. And thus we see, that *foreigners*, by living all their lives under another government, and enjoying the privileges and protection of it, though they are bound, even in conscience, to submit to its administration, as far forth as any denison; yet do not thereby come to be *subjects or members of that common-wealth*. Nothing can make any man so, but his actually entering into it by positive engagement, and express promise and compact. This is that, which I think, concerning the beginning of political societies, and that *consent which makes any one a member* of any common-wealth.

CHAP. IX.

Of the Ends of Political Society and Government.

§. 123. IF man in the state of nature be so free, as has been said; if he be absolute lord of his own person and possessions, equal to the greatest, and subject to no body, why will he part with his freedom? why will he give up this empire, and subject himself to the dominion and controul of any other power? To which it is obvious to answer,

that though in the state of nature he hath such a right, yet the enjoyment of it is very uncertain, and constantly exposed to the invasion
of others: for all being kings as much as he, every man his equal,
and the greater part no strict observers of equity and justice, the enjoyment of the property he has in this state is very unsafe, very
unsecure. This makes him willing to quit a condition, which,
however free, is full of fears and continual dangers: and it is not
without reason, that he seeks out, and is willing to join in society
with others, who are already united, or have a mind to unite, for
the mutual *preservation* of their lives, liberties and estates, which I
call by the general name, *property*.

§. 124. The great and *chief end*, therefore, of men's uniting into
common-wealths, and putting themselves under government, *is the
preservation of their property*. To which in the state of nature there
are many things wanting.

First, There wants an *established*, settled, known *law*, received
and allowed by common consent to be the standard of right and
wrong, and the common measure to decide all controversies between them: for though the law of nature be plain and intelligible to
all rational creatures; yet men being biassed by their interest, as well
as ignorant for want of study of it, are not apt to allow of it as a law
binding to them in the application of it to their particular cases.

§. 125. *Secondly*, In the state of nature there wants a *known and
indifferent judge*, with authority to determine all differences according to the established law: for every one in that state being both
judge and executioner of the law of nature, men being partial to
themselves, passion and revenge is very apt to carry them too far,
and with too much heat, in their own cases; as well as negligence,
and unconcernedness, to make them too remiss in other men's.

§. 126. *Thirdly*, In the state of nature there often wants *power* to
back and support the sentence when right, and to *give* it due *execution*. They who by any injustice offended, will seldom fail, where
they are able, by force to make good their injustice; such resistance
many times makes the punishment dangerous, and frequently
destructive, to those who attempt it.

§. 127. Thus mankind, notwithstanding all the privileges of the
state of nature, being but in an ill condition, while they remain in it,
are quickly driven into society. Hence it comes to pass, that we
seldom find any number of men live any time together in this state.
The inconveniencies that they are therein exposed to, by the irregular and uncertain exercise of the power every man has of

punishing the transgressions of others, make them take sanctuary under the established laws of government, and therein seek *the preservation of their property.* It is this makes them so willingly give up every one his single power of punishing, to be exercised by such alone, as shall be appointed to it amongst them; and by such rules as the community, or those authorized by them to that purpose, shall agree on. And in this we have the original *right and rise of both the legislative and executive power,* as well as of the governments and societies themselves.

§. 128. For in the state of nature, to omit the liberty he has of innocent delights, a man has two powers.

The first is to do whatsoever he thinks fit for the preservation of himself, and others within the permission of the *law of nature:* by which law, common to them all, he and all the rest of *mankind are one community,* make up one society, distinct from all other creatures. And were it not for the corruption and vitiousness of degenerate men, there would be no need of any other; no necessity that men should separate from this great and natural community, and by positive agreements combine into smaller and divided associations.

The other power a man has in the state of nature, is the *power to punish the crimes* committed against that law. Both these he gives up, when he joins in a private, if I may so call it, or particular politic society, and incorporates into any common-wealth, separate from the rest of mankind.

§. 129. The first *power, viz. of doing whatsoever he thought for the preservation of himself,* and the rest of mankind, *he gives up* to be regulated by laws made by the society, so far forth as the preservation of himself, and the rest of that society shall require; which laws of the society in many things confine the liberty he had by the law of nature.

§. 130. *Secondly,* The *power of punishing he wholly gives up,* and engages his natural force, (which he might before employ in the execution of the law of nature, by his own single authority, as he thought fit) to assist the executive power of the society, as the law thereof shall require: for being now in a new state, wherein he is to enjoy many conveniencies, from the labour, assistance, and society of others in the same community, as well as protection from its whole strength; he is to part also with as much of his natural liberty, in providing for himself, as the good, prosperity, and safety of the society shall require; which is not only necessary, but just, since the other members of the society do the like.

§. 131. But though men, when they enter into society, give up the equality, liberty, and executive power they had in the state of nature, into the hands of the society, to be so far disposed of by the legislative, as the good of the society shall require; yet it being only with an intention in every one the better to preserve himself, his liberty and property; (for no rational creature can be supposed to change his condition with an intention to be worse) the power of the society, or *legislative* constituted by them, can *never be supposed to extend farther, than the common good;* but is obliged to secure every one's property, by providing against those three defects above mentioned, that made the state of nature so unsafe and uneasy. And so whoever has the legislative or supreme power of any common-wealth, is bound to govern by established *standing laws,* promulgated and known to the people, and not by extemporary decrees; by *indifferent* and upright *judges,* who are to decide controversies by those laws; and to employ the force of the community at home, *only in the execution of such laws,* or abroad to prevent or redress foreign injuries, and secure the community from inroads and invasion. And all this to be directed to no other *end,* but the *peace, safety,* and *public good* of the people.

CHAP. X.

Of the Forms of a Common-wealth.

§. 132. THE majority having, as has been shewed, upon men's first uniting into society, the whole power of the community naturally in them, may employ all that power in making laws for the community from time to time, and executing those laws by officers of their own appointing; and then the *form* of the government is a perfect *democracy:* or else may put the power of making laws into the hands of a few select men, and their heirs or successors; and then it is an *oligarchy:* or else into the hands of one man, and then it is a *monarchy:* if to him and his heirs, it is an *hereditary monarchy:* if to him only for life, but upon his death the power only of nominating a successor to return to them; an *elective monarchy.* And so accordingly of these the community may make compounded and mixed forms of government, as they think good. And if the legislative power be at first given by the majority to one or more persons only for their lives, or any limited time, and then the supreme power to revert to them again; when it is so reverted, the community may dispose of it again anew into what hands they please, and so constitute a new form of government: for the *form of government depending upon the placing the* supreme power, which is *the legislative*, it being impossible to conceive that an inferior power should prescribe to a superior, or any but the supreme make laws, according as the power of making laws is placed, such is the *form of the common-wealth.*

§. 133. By *common-wealth*, I must be understood all along to mean, not a democracy, or any form of government, but *any independent community*, which the *Latines* signified by the word *civitas*, to which the word which best answers in our language, is *common-wealth*, and most properly expresses such a society of men, which community or city in *English* does not; for there may be subordinate communities in a government; and city amongst us has a quite different notion from common-wealth: and therefore, to avoid ambiguity, I crave leave to use the word *common-wealth* in that sense, in which I find it used by king *James the first*; and I take it to be its genuine signification; which if any body dislike, I consent with him to change it for a better.

CHAP. XI.

Of the Extent of the Legislative Power.

§. 134. THE great end of men's entering into society, being the enjoyment of their properties in peace and safety, and the great instrument and means of that being the laws established in that society; the *first and fundamental positive law* of all common-wealths *is the establishing of the legislative* power; as the *first and fundamental natural law*, which is to govern even the legislative itself, *is the preservation of the society*, and (as far as will consist with the public good) of every person in it. This *legislative* is not only *the supreme power* of the common-wealth, but sacred and unalterable in the hands where the community have once placed it; nor can any edict of any body else, in what form soever conceived, or by what power soever backed, have the force and obligation of a *law*, which has not its *sanction from* that *legislative* which the public has chosen and appointed: for without this the law could not have that,

which is absolutely necessary to its being a *law*, * *the consent of the
society*, over whom no body can have a power to make laws, but
by their own consent, and by authority received from them; and
therefore all the *obedience*, which by the most solemn ties any one
can be obliged *to* pay, ultimately terminates in this *supreme power*,
and is directed by those laws which it enacts: nor can any oaths to
any foreign power whatsoever, or any domestic subordinate power,
discharge any member of the society from his *obedience to the
legislative*, acting pursuant to their trust; nor oblige him to any obedience contrary to the laws so enacted, or farther than they do
allow; it being ridiculous to imagine one can be tied ultimately to
obey any *power* in the society, which is not the *supreme*.

§. 135. Though the *legislative*, whether placed in one or more,
whether it be always in being, or only by intervals, though it be the
supreme power in every common-wealth; yet,

First, It is *not*, nor can possibly be absolutely *arbitrary* over the
lives and fortunes of the people: for it being but the joint power of
every member of the society given up to that person, or assembly,
which is legislator; it can be no more than those persons had in a
state of nature before they entered into society, and gave up to the
community: for no body can transfer to another more power than
he has in himself; and no body has an absolute arbitrary power over
himself, or over any other, to destroy his own life, or take away the
life or property of another. A man, as has been proved, cannot subject himself to the arbitrary power of another; and having in the
state of nature no arbitrary power over the life, liberty, or possession of another, but only so much as the law of nature gave him for
the preservation of himself, and the rest of mankind; this is all he
doth, or can give up to the common-wealth, and by it to the

---

*The lawful power of making laws to command whole politic societies of men,
belonging so properly unto the same intire societies, that for any prince or poten-
tate of what kind soever upon earth, to exercise the same of himself, and not by express commission immediately and personally received from God, or else by
authority derived at the first from their consent, upon whose persons they impose
laws, it is no better than mere tyranny. Laws they are not therefore which public
approbation hath not made so. *Hooker's Eccl. Pol. l.* i. *sect.* 10. Of this point
therefore we are to note, that sith men naturally have no full and perfect power to
command whole politic multitudes of men, therefore utterly without our consent,
we could in such sort be at no man's commandment living. And to be commanded
we do consent, when that society, whereof we be a part, hath at any time before
consented, without revoking the same after by the like universal agreement.

Laws therefore human, of what kind so ever, are available by consent. *Ibid.*

legislative power, so that the legislative can have no more than this. Their power, in the utmost bounds of it, is *limited to the public good* of the society. It is a power, that hath no other end but preservation, and therefore can never* have a right to destroy, enslave, or designedly to impoverish the subjects. The obligations of the law of nature cease not in society, but only in many cases are drawn closer, and have by human laws known penalties annexed to them, to inforce their observation. Thus the law of nature stands as an eternal rule to all men, legislators as well as others. The *rules* that they make for other men's actions, must, as well as their own and other men's actions, be conformable to the law of nature, *i. e.* to the will of God, of which that is a declaration, and the *fundamental law of nature being the preservation of mankind*, no human sanction can be good, or valid against it.

§. 136. *Secondly,* * The *legislative*, or supreme authority, cannot assume to its self a power to rule by extemporary arbitrary decrees, but *is bound to dispense justice*, and decide the rights of the subject *by promulgated standing laws, and known authorized judges:* for the law of nature being unwritten, and so no where to be found but in the minds of men, they who through passion or interest shall miscite, or misapply it, cannot so easily be convinced of their

---

*Two foundations there are which bear up public societies; the one a natural inclination, whereby all men desire sociable life and fellowship; the other an order, expresly or secretly agreed upon, touching the manner of their union in living together: the latter is that which we call the law of a common-weal, the very soul of a politic body, the parts whereof are by law animated, held together, and set on work in such actions as the common good requireth. Laws politic, ordained for external order and regiment amongst men, are never framed as they should be, unless presuming the will of man to be inwardly obstinate, rebellious, and averse from all obedience to the sacred laws of his nature; in a word, unless presuming man to be, in regard of his depraved mind, little better than a wild beast, they do accordingly provide, notwithstanding, so to frame his outward actions, that they be no hindrance unto the common good, for which societies are instituted. Unless they do this, they are not perfect. *Hooker's Eccl. Pol. l.* i. *sect.* 10.

*Human laws are measures in respect of men whose actions they must direct, howbeit such measures they are as have also their higher rules to be measured by, which rules are two, the law of God, and the law of nature; so that laws human must be made according to the general laws of nature, and without contradiction to any positive law of scripture, otherwise they are ill made. *Hooker's Eccl. Pol. l.* iii. *sect.* 9.

To constrain men to any thing inconvenient doth seem unreasonable. *Ibid. l.* i. *sect.* 10.

mistake where there is no established judge: and so it serves not, as it ought, to determine the rights, and fence the properties of those that live under it, especially where every one is judge, interpreter, and executioner of it too, and that in his own case: and he that has right on his side, having ordinarily but his own single strength, hath not force enough to defend himself from injuries, or to punish delinquents. To avoid these inconveniences, which disorder men's properties in the state of nature, men unite into societies, that they may have the united strength of the whole society to secure and defend their properties, and may have *standing rules* to bound it, by which every one may know what is his. To this end it is that men give up all their natural power to the society which they enter into, and the community put the legislative power into such hands as they think fit, with this trust, that they shall be governed by *declared laws*, or else their peace, quiet, and property will still be at the same uncertainty, as it was in the state of nature.

§. 137. Absolute arbitrary power, or governing without *settled standing laws*, can neither of them consist with the ends of society and government, which men would not quit the freedom of the state of nature for, and tie themselves up under, were it not to preserve their lives, liberties and fortunes, and by *stated rules* of right and property to secure their peace and quiet. It cannot be supposed that they should intend, had they a power so to do, to give to any one, or more, an *absolute arbitrary power* over their persons and estates, and put a force into the magistrate's hand to execute his unlimited will arbitrarily upon them. This were to put themselves into a worse condition than the state of nature, wherein they had a liberty to defend their right against the injuries of others, and were upon equal terms of force to maintain it, whether invaded by a single man, or many in combination. Whereas by supposing they have given up themselves to the *absolute arbitrary power* and will of a legislator, they have disarmed themselves, and armed him, to make a prey of them when he pleases; he being in a much worse condition, who is exposed to the arbitrary power of one man, who has the command of 100,000, than he that is exposed to the arbitrary power of 100,000 single men; no body being secure, that his will, who has such a command, is better than that of other men, though his force be 100,000 times stronger. And therefore, whatever form the common-wealth is under, the ruling power ought to govern by *declared* and *received laws*, and not by extemporary dictates and undetermined resolutions: for then mankind

will be in a far worse condition than in the state of nature, if they
shall have armed one, or a few men with the joint power of a
multitude, to force them to obey at pleasure the exorbitant and
unlimited decrees of their sudden thoughts, or unrestrained, and till
that moment unknown wills, without having any measures set
down which may guide and justify their actions: for all the power
the government has, being only for the good of the society, as it
ought not to be *arbitrary* and at pleasure, so it ought to be exercised
by *established and promulgated laws;* that both the people may
know their duty, and be safe and secure within the limits of the law;
and the rulers too kept within their bounds, and not be tempted, by
the power they have in their hands, to employ it to such purposes,
and by such measures, as they would not have known, and own not
willingly.

§. 138. *Thirdly,* The *supreme power cannot take* from any man
any part of his *property* without his own consent: for the preservation of property being the end of government, and that for which
men enter into society, it necessarily supposes and requires, that the
people should *have property*, without which they must be supposed
to lose that, by entering into society, which was the end for which
they entered into it; too gross an absurdity for any man to own.
Men therefore *in society having property*, they have such a right to
the goods, which by the law of the community are their's, that no
body hath a right to take their substance or any part of it from
them, without their own consent: without this they have no *property* at all; for I have truly no *property* in that, which another can by
right take from me, when he pleases, against my consent. Hence it is
a mistake to think, that the *supreme or legislative power* of any
common-wealth, can do what it will, and dispose of the estates of
the subject *arbitrarily,* or take any part of them at pleasure. This is
not much to be feared in governments where the *legislative* consists,
wholly or in part, in assemblies which are variable, whose
members, upon the dissolution of the assembly, are subjects under
the common laws of their country, equally with the rest. But in
governments, where the *legislative* is in one lasting assembly always
in being, or in one man, as in absolute monarchies, there is danger
still, that they will think themselves to have a distinct interest from
the rest of the community; and so will be apt to increase their own
riches and power, by taking what they think fit from the people: for
a man's *property* is not at all secure, tho' there be good and
equitable laws to set the bounds of it between him and his fellow

subjects, if he who commands those subjects have power to take from any private man, what part he pleases of his *property*, and use and dispose of it as he thinks good.

§. 139. But *government*, into whatsoever hands it is put, being, as I have before shewed, intrusted with this condition, and *for this end*, that men might have and secure their *properties*; the prince, or senate, however it may have power to make laws, for the regulating of *property* between the subjects one amongst another, yet can never have a power to take to themselves the whole, or any part of the subjects *property*, without their own consent: for this would be in effect to leave them no *property* at all. And to let us see, that even *absolute power*, where it is necessary, is *not arbitrary* by being absolute, but is still limited by that reason, and confined to those ends, which required it in some cases to be absolute, we need look no farther than the common practice of martial discipline: for the preservation of the army, and in it of the whole common-wealth, requires an *absolute obedience* to the command of every superior officer, and it is justly death to disobey or dispute the most dangerous or unreasonable of them; but yet we see, that neither the serjeant, that could command a soldier to march up to the mouth of a cannon, or stand in a breach, where he is almost sure to perish, can command that soldier to give him one penny of his money; nor the *general*, that can condemn him to death for deserting his post, or for not obeying the most desperate orders, can yet, with all his *absolute power* of life and death, dispose of one farthing of that soldier's estate, or seize one jot of his goods; whom yet he can command any thing, and hang for the least disobedience; because such a blind obedience is necessary to that end, for which the commander has his power, *viz.* the preservation of the rest; but the disposing of his goods has nothing to do with it.

§. 140. It is true, governments cannot be supported without great charge, and it is fit every one who enjoys his share of the protection, should pay out of his estate his proportion for the maintenance of it. But still it must be with his own consent, *i. e.* the consent of the majority, giving it either by themselves, or their representatives chosen by them: for if any one shall claim a *power to lay* and levy *taxes* on the people, by his own authority, and without such consent of the people, he thereby invades the *fundamental law of property*, and subverts the end of government: for what property have I in that, which another may by right take, when he pleases, to himself?

§. 141. *Fourthly*, The *legislative cannot transfer the power of making laws* to any other hands: for it being but a delegated power from the people, they who have it cannot pass it over to others. The people alone can appoint the form of the common-wealth, which is by constituting the legislative, and appointing in whose hands that shall be. And when the people have said, We will submit to rules, and be governed by *laws* made by such men, and in such forms, no body else can say other men shall make *laws* for them; nor can the people be bound by any *laws*, but such as are enacted by those whom they have chosen, and authorized to make *laws* for them. The power of the *legislative*, being derived from the people by a positive voluntary grant and institution, can be no other than what that positive grant conveyed, which being only to make *laws*, and not to make *legislators*, the *legislative* can have no power to transfer their authority of making laws, and place it in other hands.

§. 142. These are the *bounds* which the trust, that is put in them by the society, and the law of God and nature, have *set to the legislative* power of every common-wealth, in all forms of government.

First, They are to govern by *promulgated established laws*, not to be varied in particular cases, but to have one rule for rich and poor, for the favourite at court, and the country man at plough.

Secondly, These *laws* also ought to be designed *for* no other end ultimately, but *the good of the people*.

Thirdly, They must *not raise taxes* on the *property of the people, without the consent of the people*, given by themselves, or their deputies. And this properly concerns only such governments where the *legislative* is always in being, or at least where the people have not reserved any part of the legislative to deputies, to be from time to time chosen by themselves.

Fourthly, The *legislative* neither must *nor can transfer the power of making laws* to any body else, or place it any where, but where the people have.

CHAP. XII.

Of the Legislative, Executive, and Federative
Power of the Common-wealth.

§. 143. THE *legislative* power is that, which has a right *to direct how the force of the common-wealth* shall be employed for preserving the community and the members of it. But because those laws which are constantly to be executed, and whose force is always to continue, may be made in a little time; therefore there is no need, that the *legislative* should be always in being, not having always business to do. And because it may be too great a temptation to human frailty, apt to grasp at power, for the same persons, who have the power of making laws, to have also in their hands the power to execute them, whereby they may exempt themselves from obedience to the laws they make, and suit the law, both in its making, and execution, to their own private advantage, and thereby come to have a distinct interest from the rest of the community, contrary to the end of society and government: therefore in well-ordered common-wealths, where the good of the whole is so considered, as it ought, the *legislative* power is put into the hands of divers persons, who duly assembled, have by themselves, or jointly with others, a power to make laws, which when they have done, being separated again, they are themselves subject to the laws they have made; which is a new and near tie upon them, to take care, that they make them for the public good.

§. 144. But because the laws, that are at once, and in a short time made, have a constant and lasting force, and need a *perpetual execution*, or an attendance thereunto; therefore it is necessary there should be a *power always in being*, which should see to the *execution* of the laws that are made, and remain in force. And thus the *legislative* and *executive power* come often to be separated.

§. 145. There is another *power* in every common-wealth, which one may call *natural*, because it is that which answers to the power every man naturally had before he entered into society: for though in a common-wealth the members of it are distinct persons still in reference to one another, and as such as governed by the laws of the society; yet in reference to the rest of mankind, they make one body, which is, as every member of it before was, still in the state of nature with the rest of mankind. Hence it is, that the controversies that happen between any man of the society with those that are out of it, are managed by the public; and an injury done to a member of their body, engages the whole in the reparation of it. So that under this consideration, the whole community is one body in the state of nature, in respect of all other states or persons out of its community.

§. 146. This therefore contains the power of war and peace, leagues and alliances, and all the transactions, with all persons and communities without the common-wealth, and may be called *federative*, if any one pleases. So the thing be understood, I am indifferent as to the name.

§. 147. These two powers, *executive* and *federative*, though they be really distinct in themselves, yet one comprehending the *execution* of the municipal laws of the society *within* its self, upon all that are parts of it; the other the management of the *security and interest of the public without*, with all those that it may receive benefit or damage from, yet they are always almost united. And though this *federative power* in the well or ill management of it be of great moment to the common-wealth, yet it is much less capable to be directed by antecedent, standing, positive laws, than the *executive;* and so must necessarily be left to the prudence and wisdom of those, whose hands it is in, to be managed for the public good: for the *laws* that concern subjects one amongst another, being to direct their actions, may well enough *precede* them. But what is to be done in reference to *foreigners,* depending much upon their actions, and the variation of designs and interests, must be *left* in great part *to* the *prudence* of those, who have this power committed to them, to be managed by the best of their skill, for the advantage of the common-wealth.

§. 148. Though, as I said, the *executive* and *federative power* of every community be really distinct in themselves, yet they are hardly to be separated, and placed at the same time, in the hands of distinct persons: for both of them requiring the force of the society for their exercise, it is almost impracticable to place the force of the common-wealth in distinct, and not subordinate hands; or that the *executive* and *federative power* should be *placed* in persons, that might act separately, whereby the force of the public would be under different commands: which would be apt some time or other to cause disorder and ruin.

CHAP. XIII.

Of the Subordination of the Powers of the Common-wealth.

§. 149. THOUGH in a constituted common-wealth, standing upon its own basis, and acting according to its own nature, that is, acting for the preservation of the community, there can be but *one supreme power*, which is *the legislative*, to which all the rest are and must be subordinate, yet the legislative being only a fiduciary power to act for certain ends, there remains still *in the people a supreme power to remove or alter the legislative,* when they find the *legislative* act contrary to the trust reposed in them: for all *power given with trust* for the attaining an *end,* being limited by that end, whenever that *end* is manifestly neglected, or opposed, the *trust* must necessarily be *forfeited,* and the power devolve into the hands of those that gave it, who may place it anew where they shall think best for their safety and security. And thus the *community* perpetually *retains a supreme power* of saving themselves from the attempts and designs of any body, even of their legislators, whenever they shall be so foolish, or so wicked, as to lay and carry on designs against the liberties and properties of the subject: for no man or society of men, having a power to deliver up their *preservation,* or consequently the means of it, to the absolute will and arbitrary dominion of another; when ever any one shall go about to bring them into such a slavish condition, they will always have a right to preserve, what they have not a power to part with; and to rid themselves of those, who invade this fundamental, sacred, and unalterable law of *self-preservation,* for which they entered into society. And thus the *community* may be said in this respect to be *always the supreme power,* but not as considered under any form of government, because this power of the people can never take place till the government be dissolved.

§. 150. In all cases, whilst the government subsists, the *legislative is the supreme power:* for what can give laws to another, must needs be superior to him; and since the legislative is no otherwise legislative of the society, but by the right it has to make laws for all the parts, and for every member of the society, prescribing rules to their actions, and giving power of execution, where they are transgressed, the *legislative* must needs be the *supreme,* and all other powers, in any members or parts of the society, derived from and subordinate to it.

§. 151. In some common-wealths, where the *legislative* is not always in being, and the *executive* is vested in a single person, who has also a share in the legislative; there that single person in a very tolerable sense may also be called *supreme:* not that he has in himself all the supreme power, which is that of law-making; but because he has in him the *supreme execution,* from whom all inferior magistrates derive all their several subordinate powers, or at least the greatest part of them: having also no legislative superior to him, there being no law to be made without his consent, which cannot be expected should ever subject him to the other part of the

legislative, *he* is properly enough in this sense *supreme*. But yet it is
to be observed, that tho' *oaths of allegiance* and fealty are taken to
him, it is not to him as supreme legislator, but as *supreme executor*
of the law, made by a joint power of him with others; *allegiance*
being nothing but an *obedience according to law*, which when he
violates, he has no right to obedience, nor can claim it otherwise
than as the public person vested with the power of the law, and so is
to be considered as the image, phantom, or representative of the
common-wealth, acted by the will of the society, declared in its
laws; and thus he has no will, no power, but that of the law. But
when he quits this representation, this public will, and acts by his
own private will, he degrades himself, and is but a single private
person without power, and without will, that has any right to *obedience*; the members owing no *obedience* but to the public will of
the society.

§. 152. The *executive power*, placed any where but in a person
that has also a share in the legislative, is visibly subordinate and accountable to it, and may be at pleasure changed and displaced; so
that it is not the *supreme executive power*, that is exempt from
subordination, but the *supreme executive power* vested in one, who
having a share in the legislative, has no distinct superior legislative
to be subordinate and accountable to, farther than he himself shall
join and consent; so that he is no more subordinate than he himself
shall think fit, which one may certainly conclude will be but very
little. Of other *ministerial and subordinate powers* in a common-
wealth, we need not speak, they being so multiplied with infinite
variety, in the different customs and constitutions of distinct
common-wealths, that it is impossible to give a particular account
of them all. Only thus much, which is necessary to our present purpose, we may take notice of concerning them, that they have no
manner of authority, any of them, beyond what is by positive grant
and commission delegated to them, and are all of them accountable
to some other power in the common-wealth.

§. 153. It is not necessary, no, nor so much as convenient, that
the *legislative* should be *always in being*; but absolutely necessary
that the executive power should, because there is not always need of
new laws to be made, but always need of execution of the laws that
are made. When the *legislative* hath put the *execution* of the laws,
they make, into other hands, they have a power still to resume it
out of those hands, when they find cause, and to punish for any
mal-administration against the laws. The same holds also in regard

of the *federative* power, that and the *executive* being both *ministerial* and *subordinate to the legislative*, which, as has been shewed, in a constituted common-wealth is the supreme. The *legislative* also in this case being supposed to consist of several persons, (for if it be a single person, it cannot but be always in being, and so will, as supreme, naturally have the supreme executive power, together with the legislative) may *assemble, and exercise their legislature*, at the times that either their original constitution, or their own adjournment, appoints, or when they please; if neither of these hath appointed any time, or there be no other way prescribed to convoke them: for the supreme power being placed in them by the people, it is always in them, and they may exercise it when they please, unless by their original constitution they are limited to certain seasons, or by an act of their supreme power they have adjourned to a certain time; and when that time comes, they have a right to *assemble* and act again.

§. 154. If the *legislative*, or any part of it, be made up of *representatives* chosen for that time by the people, which afterwards return into the ordinary state of subjects, and have no share in the legislature but upon a new choice, this power of chusing must also be exercised by the people, either at certain appointed seasons, or else when they are summoned to it; and in this latter case, the power of convoking the legislative is ordinarily placed in the executive, and has one of these two limitations in respect of time: that either the original constitution requires their *assembling* and *acting* at certain intervals, and then the executive power does nothing but ministerially issue directions for their electing and assembling, according to due forms; or else it is left to his prudence to call them by new elections, when the occasions or exigencies of the public require the amendment of old, or making of new laws, or the redress or prevention of any inconveniencies, that lie on, or threaten the people.

§. 155. It may be demanded here, What if the executive power, being possessed of the force of the common-wealth, shall make use of that force to hinder the *meeting* and *acting of the legislative*, when the original constitution, or the public exigencies require it? I say, using force upon the people without authority, and contrary to the trust put in him that does so, is a state of war with the people, who have a right to *reinstate* their *legislative in the exercise* of their power: for having erected a legislative, with an intent they should exercise the power of making laws, either at certain set times, or when there is need of it, when they are hindered by any force from what is so necessary to the society, and wherein the safety and preservation of the people consists, the people have a right to remove it by force. In all states and conditions, the true remedy of *force* without authority, is to oppose *force* to it. The use of *force* without authority, always puts him that uses it into a *state of war*, as the aggressor, and renders him liable to be treated accordingly.

§. 156. The *power of assembling and dismissing the legislative*, placed in the executive, gives not the executive a superiority over it, but is a fiduciary trust placed in him, for the safety of the people, in a case where the uncertainty and variableness of human affairs could not bear a steady fixed rule: for it not being possible, that the first framers of the government should, by any foresight, be so much masters of future events, as to be able to prefix so just periods of return and duration to the *assemblies of the legislative*, in all times to come, that might exactly answer all the exigencies of the common-wealth; the best remedy could be found for this defect, was to trust this to the prudence of one who was always to be present, and whose business it was to watch over the public good. Constant *frequent meetings of the legislative*, and long continuations of their assemblies, without necessary occasion, could not but be burdensome to the people, and must necessarily in time produce more dangerous inconveniencies, and yet the quick turn of affairs might be sometimes such as to need their present help: any delay of their *convening* might endanger the public; and sometimes too their business might be so great, that the limited time of their sitting might be too short for their work, and rob the public of that benefit which could be had only from their mature deliberation. What then could be done in this case to prevent the community from being exposed some time or other to eminent hazard, on one side or the other, by fixed intervals and periods, set to the *meeting and acting of the legislative*, but to intrust it to the prudence of some, who being present, and acquainted with the state of public affairs, might make use of this prerogative for the public good? and where else could this be so well placed as in his hands, who was intrusted with the execution of the laws for the same end? Thus supposing the regulation of times for the *assembling and sitting of the legislative*, not settled by the original constitution, it naturally fell into the hands of the executive, not as an arbitrary power depending on his good pleasure, but with this trust always to have it exercised only for the public weal, as the occurrences of times and change of affairs might require. Whether *settled periods of their convening*, or *a liberty* left to the prince for *convoking the legislative*, or perhaps a mixture of both, hath the least inconvenience attending it, it is not my business here to inquire, but only to shew, that though the executive power may have the prerogative of *convoking* and *dissolving* such *conventions of the legislative*, yet it is not thereby superior to it.

§. 157. Things of this world are in so constant a flux, that nothing remains long in the same state. Thus people, riches, trade, power, change their stations, flourishing mighty cities come to ruin, and prove in times neglected desolate corners, whilst other unfrequented places grow into populous countries, filled with wealth and inhabitants. But things not always changing equally, and private interest often keeping up customs and privileges, when the reasons of them are ceased, it often comes to pass, that in governments, where part of the legislative consists of *representatives* chosen by the people, that in tract of time this *representation* becomes very *unequal* and disproportionate to the reasons it was at first established upon. To what gross absurdities the following of custom, when reason has left it, may lead, we may be satisfied, when we see the bare name of a town, of which there remains not so much as the ruins, where scarce so much housing as a sheepcote, or more inhabitants than a shepherd is to be found, sends *as many representatives* to the grand assembly of law-makers, as a whole county numerous in people, and powerful in riches. This strangers stand amazed at, and every one must confess needs a remedy; tho' most think it hard to find one, because the constitution of the legislative being the original and supreme act of the society, antecedent to all positive laws in it, and depending wholly on the people, no inferior power can alter it. And therefore the *people*, when the *legislative* is once constituted, *having*, in such a government as we have been speaking of, *no power* to act as long as the government stands; this inconvenience is thought incapable of a remedy.

§. 158. *Salus populi suprema lex*, is certainly so just and fundamental a rule, that he, who sincerely follows it, cannot dangerously err. If therefore the executive, who has the power of convoking the legislative, observing rather the true proportion, than fashion of *representation*, regulates, not by old custom, but true reason, the *number of members*, in all places that have a right to be distinctly represented, which no part of the people however incorporated can pretend to, but in proportion to the assistance

which it affords to the public, it cannot be judged to have set up a
new legislative, but to have restored the old and true one, and to
have rectified the disorders which succession of time had insensibly,
as well as inevitably introduced: For it being the interest as well as
intention of the people, to have a fair and *equal representative;*
whoever brings it nearest to that, is an undoubted friend to, and
establisher of the government, and cannot miss the consent and approbation of the community; *prerogative* being nothing but a
power, in the hands of the prince, to provide for the public good, in
such cases, which depending upon unforeseen and uncertain occurrences, certain and unalterable laws could not safely direct; whatsoever shall be done manifestly for the good of the people, and the
establishing the government upon its true foundations, is, and
always will be, just *prerogative.* The power of erecting new cor-
porations, and therewith *new representatives,* carries with it a supposition, that in time the *measures of representation* might vary,
and those places have a just right to be represented which before
had none; and by the same reason, those cease to have a right, and
be too inconsiderable for such a privilege, which before had it. 'Tis
not a change from the present state, which perhaps corruption or
decay has introduced, that makes an inroad upon the government,
but the tendency of it to injure or oppress the people, and to set up
one part or party, with a distinction from, and an unequal subjection of the rest. Whatsoever cannot but be acknowledged to be of
advantage to the society, and people in general, upon just and
lasting measures, will always, when done, justify itself; and
whenever the people shall chuse their *representatives upon* just and
undeniably *equal measures,* suitable to the original frame of the
government, it cannot be doubted to be the will and act of the society, whoever permitted or caused them so to do.

CHAP. XIV.
Of PREROGATIVE.

§. 159. WHERE the legislative and executive power are in distinct
hands, (as they are in all moderated monarchies, and well-framed
governments) there the good of the society requires, that several
things should be left to the discretion of him that has the executive
power: for the legislators not being able to foresee, and provide by
laws, for all that may be useful to the community, the executor of

the laws, having the power in his hands, has by the common law of nature a right to make use of it for the good of the society, in many cases, where the municipal law has given no direction, till the legislative can conveniently be assembled to provide for it. Many things there are, which the law can by no means provide for; and those must necessarily be left to the discretion of him that has the executive power in his hands, to be ordered by him as the public good and advantage shall require: nay, it is fit that the laws themselves should in some cases give way to the executive power, or rather to this fundamental law of nature and government, *viz.* That as much as may be, *all* the members of the society are to be preserved: for since many accidents may happen, wherein a strict and rigid observation of the laws may do harm; (as not to pull down an innocent man's house to stop the fire, when the next to it is burning) and a man may come sometimes within the reach of the law, which makes no distinction of persons, by an action that may deserve reward and pardon; 'tis fit the ruler should have a power, in many cases, to mitigate the severity of the law, and pardon some offenders: for the *end of government* being *the preservation of all,* as much as may be, even the guilty are to be spared, where it can prove no prejudice to the innocent.

§. 160. This power to act according to discretion, for the public good, without the prescription of the law, and sometimes even against it, *is* that which is called *prerogative:* for since in some governments the lawmaking power is not always in being, and is usually too numerous, and so too slow, for the dispatch requisite to execution; and because also it is impossible to foresee, and so by laws to provide for, all accidents and necessities that may concern the public, or to make such laws as will do no harm, if they are executed with an inflexible rigour, on all occasions, and upon all persons that may come in their way; therefore there is a latitude left to the executive power, to do many things of choice which the laws do not prescribe.

§. 161. This power, whilst employed for the benefit of the community, and suitably to the trust and ends of the government, *is undoubted prerogative,* and never is questioned: for the people are very seldom or never scrupulous or nice in the point; they are far from examining *prerogative,* whilst it is in any tolerable degree employed for the use it was meant, that is, for the good of the people, and not manifestly against it: but if there comes to be a *question* between the executive power and the people, about a thing claimed as a *prerogative*; the tendency of the exercise of such *prerogative* to the good or hurt of the people, will easily decide that question.

§. 162. It is easy to conceive, that in the infancy of governments, when common-wealths differed little from families in number of people, they differed from them too but little in number of laws: and the governors, being as the fathers of them, watching over them for their good, the government was almost all *prerogative*. A few established laws served the turn, and the discretion and care of the ruler supplied the rest. But when mistake or flattery prevailed with weak princes to make use of this power for private ends of their own, and not for the public good, the people were fain by express laws to get prerogative determined in those points wherein they found disadvantage from it: and thus declared *limitations of prerogative* were by the people found necessary in cases which they and their ancestors had left, in the utmost latitude, to the wisdom of those princes who made no other but a right use of it, that is, for the good of their people.

§. 163. And therefore they have a very wrong notion of government, who say, that the people have *incroached upon the prerogative*, when they have got any part of it to be defined by positive laws: for in so doing they have not pulled from the prince any thing that of right belonged to him, but only declared, that that power which they indefinitely left in his or his ancestors hands, to be exercised for their good, was not a thing which they intended him when he used it otherwise: for the end of government being the good of the community, whatsoever alterations are made in it, tending to that end, cannot be an *incroachment* upon any body, since no body in government can have a right tending to any other end: and those only are *incroachments* which prejudice or hinder the public good. Those who say otherwise, speak as if the prince had a distinct and separate interest from the good of the community, and was not made for it; the root and source from which spring almost all those evils and disorders which happen in kingly governments. And indeed, if that be so, the people under his government are not a society of rational creatures, entered into a community for their mutual good; they are not such as have set rulers over themselves, to guard, and promote that good; but are to be looked on as an herd of inferior creatures under the dominion of a master, who keeps them and works them for his own pleasure or profit. If men were so void of reason, and brutish, as to enter into society upon such terms, *prerogative* might indeed be, what some men would have it, an arbitrary power to do things hurtful to the people.

§. 164. But since a rational creature cannot be supposed, when free, to put himself into subjection to another, for his own harm; (though, where he finds a good and wise ruler, he may not perhaps think it either necessary or useful to set precise bounds to his power in all things) *prerogative* can be nothing but the people's permitting their rulers to do several things, of their own free choice, where the law was silent, and sometimes too against the direct letter of the law, for the public good; and their acquiescing in it when so done: for as a good prince, who is mindful of the trust put into his hands, and careful of the good of his people, cannot have too much *prerogative*, that is, power to do good; so a weak and ill prince, who would claim that power which his predecessors exercised without the direction of the law, as a prerogative belonging to him by right of his office, which he may exercise at his pleasure, to make or promote an interest distinct from that of the public, gives the people an occasion to claim their right, and limit that power, which, whilst it was exercised for their good, they were content should be tacitly allowed.

§. 165. And therefore he that will look into the *history of England*, will find, that *prerogative* was always *largest* in the hands of our wisest and best princes; because the people, observing the whole tendency of their actions to be the public good, contested not what was done without law to that end: or, if any human frailty or mistake (for princes are but men, made as others) appeared in some small declinations from that end; yet 'twas visible, the main of their conduct tended to nothing but the care of the public. The people therefore, finding reason to be satisfied with these princes, whenever they acted without, or contrary to the letter of the law, acquiesced in what they did, and, without the least complaint, let them inlarge their *prerogative* as they pleased, judging rightly, that they did nothing herein to the prejudice of their laws, since they acted conformable to the foundation and end of all laws, the public good.

§. 166. Such god-like princes indeed had some title to arbitrary power by that argument, that would prove absolute monarchy the best government, as that which God himself governs the universe by; because such kings partake of his wisdom and goodness. Upon this is founded that saying, That the reigns of good princes have been always most dangerous to the liberties of their people: for when their successors, managing the government with different thoughts, would draw the actions of those good rulers into precedent, and make them the standard of their *prerogative*, as if what had been done only for the good of the people was a right in them to do, for the harm of the people, if they so pleased; it has often occasioned contest, and sometimes public disorders, before the people could recover their original right, and get that to be declared not to be *prerogative*, which truly was never so; since it is impossible that any body in the society should ever have a right to do the people harm; though it be very possible, and reasonable, that the people should not go about to set any bounds to the *prerogative* of those kings, or rulers, who themselves transgressed not the bounds of the public good: for *prerogative is nothing but the power of doing public good without a rule.*

§. 167. The power of *calling parliaments* in *England*, as to precise time, place, and duration, is certainly a *prerogative* of the king, but still with this trust, that it shall be made use of for the good of the nation, as the exigencies of the times, and variety of occasions, shall require: for it being impossible to foresee which should always be the fittest place for them to assemble in, and what the best season; the choice of these was left with the executive power, as might be most subservient to the public good, and best suit the ends of parliaments.

§. 168. The old question will be asked in this matter of *prerogative*, But *who shall be judge* when this power is made a right use of? I answer: between an executive power in being, with such a prerogative, and a legislative that depends upon his will for their convening, there can be no *judge on earth*; as there can be none between the legislative and the people, should either the executive, or the legislative, when they have got the power in their hands, design, or go about to enslave or destroy them. The people have no other remedy in this, as in all other cases where they have no judge on earth, but to *appeal to heaven:* for the rulers, in such attempts, exercising a power the people never put into their hands, (who can never be supposed to consent that any body should rule over them for their harm) do that which they have not a right to do. And where the body of the people, or any single man, is deprived of their right, or is under the exercise of a power without right, and have no appeal on earth, then they have a liberty to appeal to heaven, whenever they judge the cause of sufficient moment. And therefore, though the *people cannot* be *judge,* so as to have, by the constitution of that society, any superior power, to determine and give effective sentence in the case; yet they have, by a law antecedent and paramount to all positive laws of men, reserved that ultimate determination to themselves which belongs to all mankind, where there lies no appeal on earth, *viz.* to judge, whether they have just cause to make their appeal to heaven. And this judgment they cannot part with, it being out of a man's power so to submit himself to another, as to give him a liberty to destroy him; God and nature never allowing a man so to abandon himself, as to neglect his own preservation: and since he cannot take away his own life, neither can he give another power to take it. Nor let any one think, this lays a perpetual foundation for disorder; for this operates not, till the inconveniency is so great, that the majority feel it, and are weary of it, and find a necessity to have it amended. But this the executive power, or wise princes, never need come in the danger of: and it is the thing, of all others, they have most need to avoid, as of all others the most perilous.

CHAP. XV.

Of Paternal, Political, and Despotical Power,
considered together.

§. 169. THOUGH I have had occasion to speak of these separately before, yet the great mistakes of late about government, having, as I suppose, arisen from confounding these distinct powers one with another, it may not, perhaps, be amiss to consider them here together.

§. 170. First, then, *Paternal* or *parental power* is nothing but that which parents have over their children, to govern them for the children's good, till they come to the use of reason, or a state of knowledge, wherein they may be supposed capable to understand that rule, whether it be the law of nature, or the municipal law of their country, they are to govern themselves by: capable, I say, to know it, as well as several others, who live as freemen under that law. The affection and tenderness which God hath planted in the breast of parents towards their children, makes it evident, that this is not intended to be a severe arbitrary government, but only for the help, instruction, and preservation of their offspring. But happen it as it will, there is, as I have proved, no reason why it should be thought to extend to life and death, at any time, over their children, more than over any body else; neither can there be any pretence why this *parental power* should keep the child, when grown to a man, in subjection to the will of his parents, any farther than having received life and education from his parents, obliges him to respect, honour, gratitude, assistance and support, all his life, to both father and mother. And thus, 'tis true, the *paternal* is a natural *government*, but not at all extending itself to the ends and jurisdictions of that which is political. The *power of the father doth not reach* at all to the *property* of the child, which is only in his own disposing.

§. 171. *Secondly, Political power* is that power, which every man having in the state of nature, has given up into the hands of the society, and therein to the governors, whom the society hath set over itself, with this express or tacit trust, that it shall be employed for their good, and the preservation of their property: now this *power*, which every man has *in the state of nature*, and which he parts with to the society in all such cases where the society can secure him, is to use such means, for the preserving of his own property, as he thinks good, and nature allows him; and to punish the breach of the law of nature in others, so as (according to the best of his reason) may most conduce to the preservation of himself, and the rest of mankind. So that the *end and measure of this power*, when in every man's hands in the state of nature, being the preservation of all of his society, that is, all mankind in general, it can have no other *end or measure*, when in the hands of the magistrate, but to preserve the members of that society in their lives, liberties, and possessions; and so cannot be an absolute, arbitrary power over their lives and fortunes, which are as much as possible to be preserved; but a *power to make laws*, and annex such *penalties* to them, as may tend to the preservation of the whole, by cutting off those parts, and those only, which are so corrupt, that they threaten the sound and healthy, without which no severity is lawful. And this *power has its original only from compact* and agreement, and the mutual consent of those who make up the community.

§. 172. *Thirdly, Despotical power* is an absolute, arbitrary power one man has over another, to take away his life, whenever he pleases. This is a power, which neither nature gives, for it has made no such distinction between one man and another; nor compact can convey: for man not having such an arbitrary power over his own life, cannot give another man such a power over it; but it is the *effect only of forfeiture*, which the aggressor makes of his own life, when he puts himself into the state of war with another: for having quitted reason, which God hath given to be the rule betwixt man and man, and the common bond whereby human kind is united into one fellowship and society; and having renounced the way of peace which that teaches, and made use of the force of war, to compass his unjust ends upon another, where he has no right; and so revolting from his own kind to that of beasts, by making force, which is their's, to be his rule of right, he renders himself liable to be destroyed by the injured person, and the rest of mankind, that will join with him in the execution of justice, as any other wild beast, or noxious brute, with whom mankind can have neither society nor security*. And thus *captives*, taken in a just and lawful war, and such only, are *subject to a despotical power*, which, as it arises not from compact, so neither is it capable of any, but is the state of war continued: for what compact can be made with a man that is not master of his own life? what condition can he perform? and if he be once allowed to be master of his own life, the *despotical, arbitrary power* of his master ceases. He that is master of himself, and his own life, has a right too to the means of preserving it; so that *as soon as compact enters, slavery ceases*, and he so far quits his absolute power, and puts an end to the state of war, who enters into conditions with his captive.

§. 173. *Nature gives* the first of these, *viz. paternal power to parents* for the benefit of their children during their minority, to supply their want of ability, and understanding how to manage their property. (By *property* I must be understood here, as in other places, to mean that property which men have in their persons as well as goods.) *Voluntary agreement gives* the second, *viz. political power to governors* for the benefit of their subjects, to secure them in the possession and use of their properties. And *forfeiture gives* the third *despotical power to lords* for their own benefit, over those who are stripped of all property.

§. 174. He, that shall consider the distinct rise and extent, and the different ends of these several powers, will plainly see, that *paternal power* comes as far short of that of the *magistrate*, as *despotical* exceeds it; and that *absolute dominion*, however placed, is so far from being one kind of civil society, that it is as inconsistent with it, as slavery is with property. *Paternal power* is only where minority

---

*Another copy corrected by Mr. Locke, has it thus, *Noxious brute that is destructive to their being.*

makes the child incapable to manage his property; *political,* where men have property in their own disposal; and *despotical,* over such as have no property at all.

CHAP. XVI.
Of CONQUEST.

§. 175. THOUGH governments can originally have no other rise than that before mentioned, nor *polities* be *founded on* any thing but *the consent of the people;* yet such have been the disorders ambition has filled the world with, that in the noise of war, which makes so great a part of the history of mankind, *this consent* is little taken notice of: and therefore many have mistaken the force of arms for the consent of the people, and reckon conquest as one of the originals of government. But *conquest* is as far from setting up any government, as demolishing an house is from building a new one in the place. Indeed, it often makes way for a new frame of a common-wealth, by destroying the former; but, without the consent of the people, can never erect a new one.

§. 176. That the *aggressor,* who puts himself into the state of war with another, and *unjustly invades* another man's right, *can,* by such an unjust war, *never* come to *have a right over the conquered,* will be easily agreed by all men, who will not think, that robbers and pyrates have a right of empire over whomsoever they have force enough to master; or that men are bound by promises, which unlawful force extorts from them. Should a robber break into my house, and with a dagger at my throat make me seal deeds to convey my estate to him, would this give him any title? Just such a title, by his sword, has an *unjust conqueror,* who forces me into submission. The injury and the crime is equal, whether committed by the wearer of a crown, or some petty villain. The title of the offender, and the number of his followers, make no difference in the offence, unless it be to aggravate it. The only difference is, great robbers punish little ones, to keep them in their obedience; but the great ones are rewarded with laurels and triumphs, because they are too big for the weak hands of justice in this world, and have the power in their own possession, which should punish offenders. What is my remedy against a robber, that so broke into my house? *Appeal* to the law for justice. But perhaps justice is denied, or I am crippled and cannot stir, robbed and have not the means to do it. If God has taken away all means of seeking remedy, there is nothing left but patience. But my son, when able, may seek the relief of the law, which I am denied: he or his son may renew his *appeal*, till he recover his right. But the conquered, or their children, have no court, no arbitrator on earth to appeal to. Then they may *appeal*, as *Jephtha* did, *to heaven*, and repeat their *appeal* till they have recovered the native right of their ancestors, which was, to have such a legislative over them, as the majority should approve, and freely acquiesce in. If it be objected, This would cause endless trouble; I answer, no more than justice does, where she lies open to all that appeal to her. He that troubles his neighbour without a cause, is punished for it by the justice of the court he appeals to: and he that *appeals to heaven* must be sure he has right on his side; and a right too that is worth the trouble and cost of the appeal, as he will answer at a tribunal that cannot be deceived, and will be sure to retribute to every one according to the mischiefs he hath created to his fellow subjects; that is, any part of mankind: from whence it is plain, that he that *conquers in an unjust war can thereby have no title to the subjection and obedience of the conquered.*

§.177. But supposing victory favours the right side, let us consider a *conqueror in a lawful war*, and see what power he gets, and over whom.

First, It is plain he *gets no power by his conquest over those that conquered with him.* They that fought on his side cannot suffer by the conquest, but must at least be as much freemen as they were before. And most commonly they serve upon terms, and on condition to share with their leader, and enjoy a part of the spoil, and other advantages that attend the conquering sword; or at least have a part of the subdued country bestowed upon them. And the *conquering people are not, I hope, to be slaves by conquest,* and wear their laurels only to shew they are sacrifices to their leaders triumph. They that found absolute monarchy upon the title of the sword, make their heroes, who are the founders of such monarchies, arrant *Draw-can-sirs*, and forget they had any officers and soldiers that fought on their side in the battles they won, or assisted them in the subduing, or shared in possessing, the countries they mastered. We are told by some, that the *English* monarchy is founded in the *Norman* conquest, and that our princes have thereby a title to absolute dominion: which if it were true, (as by the history it appears otherwise) and that *William* had a right to make war on this island; yet his dominion by conquest could reach no farther than to the *Saxons* and *Britons*, that were then inhabitants of this country. The *Normans* that came with him, and helped to conquer, and all descended from them, are freemen, and no subjects by conquest; let that give what dominion it will. And if I, or any body else, shall claim freedom, as derived from them, it will be very hard to prove the contrary: and it is plain, the law, that has made no distinction between the one and the other, intends not there should be any difference in their freedom or privileges.

§. 178. But supposing, which seldom happens, that the conquerors and conquered never incorporate into one people, under the same laws and freedom; let us see next *what power a lawful conqueror has over the subdued:* and that I say is purely despotical. He has an absolute power over the lives of those who by an unjust war have forfeited them; but not over the lives or fortunes of those who engaged not in the war, nor over the possessions even of those who were actually engaged in it.

§. 179. *Secondly,* I say then the *conqueror* gets no power but only over those who have actually assisted, concurred, or consented to that unjust force that is used against him: for the people having given to their governors no power to do an unjust thing, such as is to make an unjust war, (for they never had such a power in themselves) they ought not to be charged as guilty of the violence and unjustice that is committed in an unjust war, any farther than they actually abet it; no more than they are to be thought guilty of any violence or oppression their governors should use upon the people themselves, or any part of their fellow subjects, they having impowered them no more to the one than to the other. Conquerors, it is true, seldom trouble themselves to make the distinction, but they willingly permit the confusion of war to sweep all together: but yet this alters not the right; for the conquerors power over the lives of the conquered, being only because they have used force to do, or maintain an injustice, he can have that power only over those who have concurred in that force; all the rest are innocent; and he has no more title over the people of that country, who have done him no injury, and so have made no forfeiture of their lives, than he has over any other, who, without any injuries or provocations, have lived upon fair terms with him.

§. 180. *Thirdly,* The *power a conqueror gets* over those he overcomes *in a just war, is perfectly despotical:* he has an absolute power over the lives of those, who, by putting themselves in a state of war, have forfeited them; but he has not thereby a right and title to their possessions. This I doubt not, but at first sight will seem a strange doctrine, it being so quite contrary to the practice of the world; there being nothing more familiar in speaking of the dominion of countries, than to say such an one conquered it; as if conquest, without any more ado, conveyed a right of possession. But when we consider, that the practice of the strong and powerful, how universal soever it may be, is seldom the rule of right, however it be one part of the subjection of the conquered, not to argue against the conditions cut out to them by the conquering sword.

§. 181. Though in all war there be usually a complication of force and damage, and the aggressor seldom fails to harm the estate, when he uses force against the persons of those he makes war upon; yet it is the use of force only that puts a man into the state of war: for whether by force he begins the injury, or else having quietly, and by fraud, done the injury, he refuses to make reparation, and by force maintains it, (which is the same thing, as at first to have done it by force) it is the unjust use of force that makes the war: for he that breaks open my house, and violently turns me out of doors; or having peaceably got in, by force keeps me out, does in effect the same thing; supposing we are in such a state, that we have no common judge on earth, whom I may appeal to, and to whom we are both obliged to submit: for of such I am now speaking. It is the *unjust use of force* then, that *puts a man into the state of war* with another; and thereby he that is guilty of it makes a forfeiture of his life: for quitting reason, which is the rule given between man and man, and using force, the way of beasts, he becomes liable to be destroyed by him he uses force against, as any savage ravenous beast, that is dangerous to his being.

§. 182. But because the miscarriages of the father are no faults of the children, and they may be rational and peaceable, notwithstanding the brutishness and injustice of the father; the father, by his miscarriages and violence, can forfeit but his own life, but involves not his children in his guilt or destruction. His goods, which nature, that willeth the preservation of all mankind as much as is possible, hath made to belong to the children to keep them from perishing, do still continue to belong to his children: for supposing them not to have joined in the war, either thro' infancy, absence, or choice, they have done nothing to forfeit them: *nor has the conqueror any right* to take them away, by the bare title of having subdued him that by force attempted his destruction; though perhaps he may have some right to them, to repair the damages he has sus-

tained by the war, and the defence of his own right; which how far
it reaches to the possessions of the conquered, we shall see by and
by. So that he that *by conquest has a right over a man's person to*
destroy him if he pleases, has *not* thereby a right over *his estate* to
possess and enjoy it: for it is the brutal force the aggressor has used,
that gives his adversary a right to take away his life, and destroy
him if he pleases, as a noxious creature; but it is damage sustained
that alone gives him title to another man's goods: for though I may
kill a thief that sets on me in the highway, yet I may not (which
seems less) take away his money, and let him go: this would be robbery on my side. His force, and the state of war he put himself in,
made him forfeit his life, but gave me no title to his goods. The *right*
then of *conquest extends only to the lives* of those who joined in the
war, *not to their estates*, but only in order to make reparation for
the damages received, and the charges of the war, and that too with
reservation of the right of the innocent wife and children.

§. 183. Let the *conqueror* have as much justice on his side, as
could be supposed, he *has* no *right* to seize more than the vanquished could forfeit: his life is at the victor's mercy; and his service
and goods he may appropriate, to make himself reparation; but he
cannot take the goods of his wife and children; they too had a title
to the goods he enjoyed, and their shares in the estate he possessed:
for example, I in the state of nature (and all common-wealths are in
the state of nature one with another) have injured another man, and
refusing to give satisfaction, it comes to a state of war, wherein my
defending by force what I had gotten unjustly, makes me the aggressor. I am conquered: my life, it is true, as forfeit, is at mercy,
but not my wife's and children's. They made not the war, nor
assisted in it. I could not forfeit their lives; they were not mine to
forfeit. My wife had a share in my estate; that neither could I
forfeit. And my children also, being born of me, had a right to be
maintained out of my labour or substance. Here then is the case: the
conqueror has a title to reparation for damages received, and the
children have a title to their father's estate for their subsistence: for
as to the wife's share, whether her own labour, or compact, gave
her a title to it, it is plain, her husband could not forfeit what was
her's. What must be done in the case? I answer; the fundamental
law of nature being, that all, as much as may be, should be preserved, it follows, that if there be not enough fully to *satisfy* both,
viz. for the *conqueror's losses*, and children's maintenance, he that
hath, and to spare, must remit something of his full satisfaction,

and give way to the pressing and preferable title of those who are in
danger to perish without it.

§. 184. But supposing the *charge* and *damages of the war* are to
be made up to the conqueror, to the utmost farthing; and that the
children of the vanquished, spoiled of all their father's goods, are to
be left to starve and perish; yet the satisfying of what shall, on this
score, be due to the conqueror, will scarce give him a *title to any
country he shall conquer:* for the damages of war can scarce amount
to the value of any considerable tract of land, in any part of the
world, where all the land is possessed, and none lies waste. And if I
have not taken away the conqueror's land, which, being vanquished, it is impossible I should; scarce any other spoil I have done
him can amount to the value of mine, supposing it equally
cultivated, and of an extent any way coming near what I had over-
run of his. The destruction of a year's product or two (for it seldom
reaches four or five) is the utmost spoil that usually can be done: for
as to money, and such riches and treasure taken away, these are
none of nature's goods, they have but a fantastical imaginary value:
nature has put no such upon them: they are of no more account by
her standard, than the wampompeke of the *Americans* to an *Euro-
pean* prince, or the silver money of *Europe* would have been
formerly to an *American*. And five years product is not worth the
perpetual inheritance of land, where all is possessed, and none remains waste, to be taken up by him that is disseized: which will be
easily granted, if one do but take away the imaginary value of
money, the disproportion being more than between five and five
hundred; though, at the same time, half a year's product is more
worth than the inheritance, where there being more land than the
inhabitants possess and make use of, any one has liberty to make
use of the waste: but there conquerors take little care to possess
themselves of the *lands of the vanquished*. No damage therefore,
that men in the state of nature (as all princes and governments are in
reference to one another) suffer from one another, can give a conqueror power to dispossess the posterity of the vanquished, and
turn them out of that inheritance, which ought to be the possession
of them and their descendants to all generations. The conqueror indeed will be apt to think himself master: and it is the very condition
of the subdued not to be able to dispute their right. But if that be all,
it gives no other title than what bare force gives to the stronger over
the weaker: and, by this reason, he that is strongest will have a right
to whatever he pleases to seize on.

§. 185. Over those then that joined with him in the war, and over those of the subdued country that opposed him not, and the posterity even of those that did, the conqueror, even in a just war, hath, by his conquest, no *right of dominion:* they are free from any subjection to him, and if their former government be dissolved, they are at liberty to begin and erect another to themselves.

§. 186. The conqueror, it is true, usually, by the force he has over them, compels them, with a sword at their breasts, to stoop to his conditions, and submit to such a government as he pleases to afford them; but the enquiry is, what right he has to do so? If it be said, they submit by their own consent, then this allows their own *consent* to be *necessary to give the conqueror a title to rule* over them. It remains only to be considered, whether *promises extorted by force,* without right, can be thought consent, and *how far they bind.* To which I shall say, they *bind not at all;* because whatsoever another gets from me by force, I still retain the right of, and he is obliged presently to restore. He that forces my horse from me, ought presently to restore him, and I have still a right to retake him. By the same reason, he that *forced a promise* from me, ought presently to restore it, *i. e.* quit me of the obligation of it; or I may resume it myself, *i. e.* chuse whether I will perform it: for the law of nature laying an obligation on me only by the rules she prescribes, cannot oblige me by the violation of her rules: such is the extorting any thing from me by force. Nor does it at all alter the case to say, *I gave my promise,* no more than it excuses the force, and passes the right, when I put my hand in my pocket, and deliver my purse myself to a thief, who demands it with a pistol at my breast.

§. 187. From all which it follows, that the *government of a conqueror,* imposed by force on the subdued, against whom he had no right of war, or who joined not in the war against him, where he had right, *has no obligation* upon them.

§. 188. But let us suppose, that all the men of that community, being all members of the same body politic, may be taken to have joined in that unjust war wherein they are subdued, and so their lives are at the mercy of the conqueror.

§. 189. I say, this concerns not their children who are in their minority: for since a father hath not, in himself, a power over the life or liberty of his child, no act of his can possibly forfeit it. So that the children, whatever may have happened to the fathers, are freemen, and the absolute power of the *conqueror* reaches no farther than the persons of the men that were subdued by him, and dies with them: and should he govern them as slaves, subjected to his absolute arbitrary power, he *has* no *such right of dominion over their children*. He can have no power over them but by their own consent, whatever he may drive them to say or do; and he has no lawfull authority, whilst force, and not choice, compels them to submission.

§. 190. Every man is born with a double right: *first*, a *right of freedom to his person*, which no other man has a power over, but the free disposal of it lies in himself. *Secondly*, a *right*, before any other man, *to inherit* with his brethren his *father's goods*.

§. 191. By the first of these, a man is *naturally free* from subjection to any government, tho' he be born in a place under its jurisdiction; but if he disclaim the lawful government of the country he was born in, he must also quit the right that belonged to him by the laws of it, and the possessions there descending to him from his ancestors, if it were a government made by their consent.

§. 192. By the second, the *inhabitants* of any country, who are descended, and derive a title to their estates from those who are subdued, and had a government forced upon them against their free consents, *retain a right to the possession of their ancestors*, though they consent not freely to the government, whose hard conditions were by force imposed on the possessors of that country: for the first *conqueror never having had a title to the land* of that country, the people who are the descendants of, or claim under those who were forced to submit to the yoke of a government by constraint, have always a right to shake it off, and free themselves from the usurpation or tyranny which the sword hath brought in upon them, till their rulers put them under such a frame of government as they willingly and of choice consent to. Who doubts but the Grecian christians, descendants of the ancient possessors of that country, may justly cast off the Turkish yoke, which they have so long groaned under, whenever they have an opportunity to do it? For no government can have a right to obedience from a people who have not freely consented to it; which they can never be supposed to do, till either they are put in a full state of liberty to chuse their government and governors, or at least till they have such standing laws, to which they have by themselves or their representatives given their free consent, and also till they are allowed their due property, which is so to be proprietors of what they have, that no body can take away any part of it without their own consent, without which, men under any government are not in the state of freemen, but are direct slaves under the force of war.

§. 193. But granting that the *conqueror* in a just war has a right to the estates, as well as power over the persons, of the conquered; which, it is plain, he *hath* not: nothing of *absolute power* will follow from hence, in the continuance of the government; because the descendants of these being all freemen, if he grants them estates and possessions to inhabit his country, (without which it would be worth nothing) whatsoever he grants them, they have, so far as it is granted, *property* in. The nature whereof is, that *without a man's own consent it cannot be taken from him.*

§. 194. Their *persons* are *free* by a native right, and their *properties*, be they more or less, are *their own, and at their own dispose*, and not at his; or else it is no *property*. Supposing the conqueror gives to one man a thousand acres, to him and his heirs for ever; to another he lets a thousand acres for his life, under the rent of 50l. or 500l. *per ann.* has not the one of these a right to his thousand acres for ever, and the other, during his life, paying the said rent? and hath not the tenant for life a *property* in all that he gets over and above his rent, by his labour and industry during the said term, supposing it be double the rent? Can any one say, the king, or conqueror, after his grant, may by his power of conqueror take away all, or part of the land from the heirs of one, or from the other during his life, he paying the rent? or can he take away from either the goods or money they have got upon the said land, at his pleasure? If he can, then all free and voluntary *contracts* cease, and are void in the world; there needs nothing to dissolve them at any time, but power enough: and all the *grants* and *promises* of *men in power* are but mockery and collusion: for can there be any thing more ridiculous than to say, I give you and your's this for ever, and that in the surest and most solemn way of conveyance can be devised; and yet it is to be understood, that I have right, if I please, to take it away from you again to morrow?

§. 195. I will not dispute now whether princes are exempt from the laws of their country; but this I am sure, they owe subjection to the laws of God and nature. No body, no power, can exempt them from the obligations of that eternal law. Those are so great, and so strong, in the case of *promises*, that omnipotency itself can be tied by them. *Grants, promises, and oaths, are bonds that hold the Almighty:* whatever some flatterers say to princes of the world, who all together, with all their people joined to them, are, in comparison of the great God, but as a drop of the bucket, or a dust on the balance, inconsiderable, nothing!

§. 196. The short of the *case in conquest* is this: the conqueror, if he have a just cause, has a despotical right over the persons of all, that actually aided, and concurred in the war against him, and a right to make up his damage and cost out of their labour and estates, so he injure not the right of any other. Over the rest of the people, if there were any that consented not to the war, and over the children of the captives themselves, or the possessions of either, he has no power; and so can have, *by virtue of conquest, no lawful title* himself *to dominion* over them, or derive it to his posterity; but is an aggressor, if he attempts upon their properties, and thereby puts himself in a state of war against them, and has no better a right of principality, he, nor any of his successors, than *Hingar*, or *Hubba*, the Danes, had here in *England;* or *Spartacus*, had he conquered *Italy*, would have had; which is to have their yoke cast off, as soon as God shall give those under their subjection courage and opportunity to do it. Thus, notwithstanding whatever title the kings of *Assyria* had over *Judah*, by the sword, God assisted *Hezekiah* to throw off the dominion of that conquering empire. *And the lord was with Hezekiah, and he prospered; wherefore he went forth, and he rebelled against the king of Assyria, and served him not,* 2 Kings xviii. 7. Whence it is plain, that shaking off a power, which force, and not right, hath set over any one, though it hath the name of *rebellion*, yet is no offence before God, but is that which he allows and countenances, though even promises and covenants, when obtained by force, have intervened: for it is very probable, to any one that reads the story of *Ahaz* and *Hezekiah* attentively, that the *Assyrians* subdued *Ahaz*, and deposed him, and made *Hezekiah* king in his father's lifetime; and that *Hezekiah* by agreement had done him homage, and paid him tribute all this time.

CHAP. XVII.

Of *USURPATION*.

§. 197. AS conquest may be called a foreign usurpation, so usurpation is a kind of domestic conquest, with this difference, that an usurper can never have right on his side, it being no *usurpation*, but where one is got into the *possession of what another has right to*. This, so far as it is *usurpation*, is a change only of persons, but not of the forms and rules of the government: for if the usurper extend his power beyond what of right belonged to the lawful princes, or governors of the commonwealth, it is *tyranny* added to *usurpation*.

§. 198. In all lawful governments, the designation of the persons, who are to bear rule, is as natural and necessary a part as the form of the government itself, and is that which had its establishment originally from the people; the anarchy being much alike, to have no form of government at all; or to agree, that it shall be monarchical, but to appoint no way to design the person that shall have the power, and be the monarch. Hence all commonwealths, with the form of government established, have rules also of appointing those who are to have any share in the public authority, and settled methods of conveying the right to them: for the anarchy is much alike, to have no form of government at all; or to agree that it shall be monarchical, but to appoint no way to know or design the person that shall have the power, and be the monarch. Whoever gets into the exercise of any part of the power, by other ways than what the laws of the community have prescribed, hath no right to be obeyed, though the form of the commonwealth be still preserved; since he is not the person the laws have appointed, and consequently not the person the people have consented to. Nor can such an *usurper*, or any deriving from him, ever have a title, till the people are both at liberty to consent, and have actually consented to allow, and confirm in him the power he hath till then usurped.

CHAP. XVIII.

Of TYRANNY.

§. 199. AS usurpation is the exercise of power, which another hath a right to; so *tyranny is the exercise of power beyond right*, which no body can have a right to. And this is making use of the power any one has in his hands, not for the good of those who are under it, but for his own private separate advantage. When the governor, however intitled, makes not the law, but his will, the rule; and his commands and actions are not directed to the preservation of the properties of his people, but the satisfaction of his own ambition, revenge, covetousness, or any other irregular passion.

§. 200. If one can doubt this to be truth, or reason, because it comes from the obscure hand of a subject, I hope the authority of a king will make it pass with him. King *James* the first, in his speech to the parliament, 1603, tells them thus, *I will ever prefer the weal*

*of the public, and of the whole commonwealth, in making of good
laws and constitutions, to any particular and private ends of mine;
thinking ever the wealth and weal of the commonwealth to be my
greatest weal and worldly felicity; a point wherein a lawful king
doth directly differ from a tyrant: for I do acknowledge, that the
special and greatest point of difference that is between a rightful
king and an usurping tyrant, is this, that whereas the proud and am-
bitious tyrant doth think his kingdom and people are only ordained
for satisfaction of his desires and unreasonable appetites, the
righteous and just king doth by the contrary acknowledge himself
to be ordained for the procuring of the wealth and property of his
people.* And again, in his speech to the parliament, 1609, he hath
these words, *The king binds himself by a double oath, to the observation of the fundamental laws of his kingdom; tacitly, as by being
a king, and so bound to protect as well the people, as the laws of his
kingdom; and expressly, by his oath at his coronation; so as every
just king, in a settled kingdom, is bound to observe that paction
made to his people, by his laws, in framing his government
agreeable thereunto, according to that paction which God made
with* Noah *after the deluge. Hereafter, seed-time and harvest, and
cold and heat, and summer and winter, and day and night, shall not
cease while the earth remaineth. And therefore a king governing in
a settled kingdom, leaves to be a king, and degenerates into a
tyrant, as soon as he leaves off to rule according to his laws.* And a
little after, *Therefore all kings that are not tyrants, or perjured, will
be glad to bound themselves within the limits of their laws; and they
that persuade them the contrary, are vipers, and pests both against
them and the commonwealth.* Thus that learned king, who well
understood the notion of things, makes the difference betwixt a
king and a *tyrant* to consist only in this, that one makes the laws the
bounds of his power, and the good of the public, the end of his
government; the other makes all give way to his own will and appetite.

§. 201. It is a mistake, to think this fault is proper only to monarchies; other forms of government are liable to it, as well as that: for
wherever the power, that is put in any hands for the government of
the people, and the preservation of their properties, is applied to
other ends, and made use of to impoverish, harass, or subdue them
to the arbitrary and irregular commands of those that have it; there
it presently becomes *tyranny*, whether those that thus use it are one
or many. Thus we read of the thirty tyrants at *Athens*, as well as

one at *Syracuse;* and the intolerable dominion of the *Decemviri* at *Rome* was nothing better.

§. 202. *Where-ever law ends, tyranny begins,* if the law be transgressed to another's harm; and whosoever in authority exceeds the power given him by the law, and makes use of the force he has under his command, to compass that upon the subject, which the law allows not, ceases in that to be a magistrate; and, acting without authority, may be opposed, as any other man, who by force invades the right of another. This is acknowledged in subordinate magistrates. He that hath authority to seize my person in the street, may be opposed as a thief and a robber, if he endeavours to break into my house to execute a writ, notwithstanding that I know he has such a warrant, and such a legal authority, as will impower him to arrest me abroad. And why this should not hold in the highest, as well as in the most inferior magistrate, I would gladly be informed. Is it reasonable, that the eldest brother, because he has the greatest part of his father's estate, should thereby have a right to take away any of his younger brothers portions? or that a rich man, who possessed a whole country, should from thence have a right to seize, when he pleased, the cottage and garden of his poor neighbour? The being rightfully possessed of great power and riches, exceedingly beyond the greatest part of the sons of *Adam*, is so far from being an excuse, much less a reason, for rapine and oppression, which the endamaging another without authority is, that it is a great aggravation of it: for the exceeding the bounds of authority is no more a right in a great, than in a petty officer; no more justifiable in a king than a constable; but is so much the worse in him, in that he has more trust put in him, has already a much greater share than the rest of his brethren, and is supposed, from the advantages of his education, employment, and counsellors, to be more knowing in the measures of right and wrong.

§. 203. May the *commands* then *of a prince be opposed?* may he be resisted as often as any one shall find himself aggrieved, and but imagine he has not right done him? This will unhinge and overturn all polities, and, instead of government and order, leave nothing but anarchy and confusion.

§. 204. To this I answer, that *force* is to be *opposed* to nothing, but to unjust and unlawful *force;* whoever makes any opposition in any other case, draws on himself a just condemnation both from God and man; and so no such danger or confusion will follow, as is often suggested: for,

§. 205. *First,* As, in some countries, the person of the prince by
the law is sacred; and so, whatever he commands or does, his person is still free from all question or violence, not liable to force, or
any judicial censure or condemnation. But yet opposition may be
made to the illegal acts of any inferior officer, or other commis-
sioned by him; unless he will, by actually putting himself into a
state of war with his people, dissolve the government, and leave
them to that defence which belongs to every one in the state of
nature: for of such things who can tell what the end will be? and a
neighbour kingdom has shewed the world an odd example. In all
other cases the *sacredness* of the *person exempts him from all inconveniencies,* whereby he is secure, whilst the government stands,
from all violence and harm whatsoever; than which there cannot be
a wiser constitution: for the harm he can do in his own person not
being likely to happen often, nor to extend itself far; nor being able
by his single strength to subvert the laws, nor oppress the body of
the people, should any prince have so much weakness, and ill
nature as to be willing to do it, the inconveniency of some particular
mischiefs, that may happen sometimes, when a heady prince comes
to the throne, are well recompensed by the peace of the public, and
security of the government, in the person of the chief magistrate,
thus set out of the reach of danger: it being safer for the body, that
some few private men should be sometimes in danger to suffer, than
that the head of the republic should be easily, and upon slight occasions, exposed.

§. 206. *Secondly,* But this privilege, belonging only to the king's
person, hinders not, but they may be questioned, opposed, and
resisted, who use unjust force, though they pretend a commission
from him, which the law authorizes not; as is plain in the case of
him that has the king's writ to arrest a man, which is a full commission from the king; and yet he that has it cannot break open a man's
house to do it, nor execute this command of the king upon certain
days, nor in certain places, though this commission have no such
exception in it; but they are the limitations of the law, which if any
one transgress, the king's commission excuses him not: for the
king's authority being given him only by the law, he cannot impower any one to act against the law, or justify him, by his commission, in so doing; the *commission,* or *command of any magistrate,
where he has no authority,* being as *void* and insignificant, as that
of any private man; the difference between the one and the other,
being that the magistrate has some authority so far, and to such

ends, and the private man has none at all: for it is not the *commis-sion*, but the *authority*, that gives the right of acting; and *against the laws there can be no authority*. But, notwithstanding such resistance, the king's person and authority are still both secured, and so *no danger to governor or government*.

§. 207. *Thirdly*, Supposing a government wherein the person of the chief magistrate is not thus sacred; yet this *doctrine* of the lawfulness of *resisting* all unlawful exercises of his power, *will not* upon every slight occasion indanger him, or *imbroil the govern-ment:* for where the injured party may be relieved, and his damages repaired by appeal to the law, there can be no pretence for force, which is only to be used where a man is intercepted from appealing to the law: for nothing is to be accounted hostile force, but where it leaves not the remedy of such an appeal; and it is such *force* alone, that *puts* him that uses it *into a state of war*, and makes it lawful to resist him. A man with a sword in his hand demands my purse in the high-way, when perhaps I have not twelve pence in my pocket: this man I may lawfully kill. To another I deliver 100l. to hold only whilst I alight, which he refuses to restore me, when I am got up again, but draws his sword to defend the possession of it by force, if I endeavour to retake it. The mischief this man does me is a hun-dred, or possibly a thousand times more than the other perhaps in-tended me (whom I killed before he really did me any); and yet I might lawfully kill the one, and cannot so much as hurt the other lawfully. The reason whereof is plain; because the one using *force*, which threatened my life, I could not have *time to appeal* to the law to secure it: and when it was gone, it was too late to appeal. The law could not restore life to my dead carcass: the loss was irreparable; which to prevent, the law of nature gave me a right to *destroy* him, who had put himself into a state of war with me, and threatened my destruction. But in the other case, my life not being in danger, I may have the *benefit of appealing* to the law, and have reparation for my 100l. that way.

§. 208. *Fourthly*, But if the unlawful acts done by the magistrate be maintained (by the power he has got), and the remedy which is due by law, be by the same power obstructed; yet the *right of resisting*, even in such manifest acts of tyranny, *will not* suddenly, or on slight occasions, *disturb the government:* for if it reach no far-ther than some private men's cases, though they have a right to de-fend themselves, and to recover by force what by unlawful force is taken from them; yet the right to do so will not easily engage them in a contest, wherein they are sure to perish; it being as impossible for one, or a few oppressed men to *disturb the government*, where the body of the people do not think themselves concerned in it, as for a raving mad-man, or heady mal-content to overturn a well-settled state; the people being as little apt to follow the one, as the other.

§. 209. But if either these illegal acts have extended to the majority of the people; or if the mischief and oppression has lighted only on some few, but in such cases, as the precedent, and consequences seem to threaten all; and they are persuaded in their consciences, that their laws, and with them their estates, liberties, and lives are in danger, and perhaps their religion too; how they will be hindered from resisting illegal force, used against them, I cannot tell. This is an *inconvenience,* I confess, *that attends all governments* whatsoever, when the governors have brought it to this pass, to be generally suspected of their people; the most dangerous state which they can possibly put themselves in; wherein they are the less to be pitied, because it is so easy to be avoided; it being as impossible for a governor, if he really means the good of his people, and the preservation of them, and their laws together, not to make them see and feel it, as it is for the father of a family, not to let his children see he loves, and takes care of them.

§. 210. But if all the world shall observe pretences of one kind, and actions of another; arts used to elude the law, and the trust of prerogative (which is an arbitrary power in some things left in the prince's hand to do good, not harm to the people) employed contrary to the end for which it was given: if the people shall find the ministers and subordinate magistrates chosen suitable to such ends, and favoured, or laid by, proportionably as they promote or oppose them: if they see several experiments made of arbitrary power, and that religion underhand favoured, (tho' publicly proclaimed against) which is readiest to introduce it; and the operators in it supported, as much as may be; and when that cannot be done, yet approved still, and liked the better: if a *long train of actions shew the councils* all tending that way; how can a man any more hinder himself from being persuaded in his own mind, which way things are going; or from casting about how to save himself, than he could from believing the captain of the ship he was in, was carrying him, and the rest of the company, to *Algiers,* when he found him always steering that course, though cross winds, leaks in his ship, and want of men and provisions did often force him to turn his course another way for some time, which he steadily returned to again, as soon as the wind, weather, and other circumstances would let him?

CHAP. XIX.

Of the Dissolution of Government.

§. 211. HE that will with any clearness speak of the *dissolution of government*, ought in the first place to distinguish between the *dissolution of the society* and the *dissolution of the government.* That which makes the community, and brings men out of the loose state of nature, into *one politic society*, is the agreement which every one has with the rest to incorporate, and act as one body, and so be one distinct common-wealth. The usual, and almost only way whereby *this union is dissolved*, is the inroad of foreign force making a conquest upon them: for in that case, (not being able to maintain and support themselves, as *one intire* and *independent body)* the union belonging to that body which consisted therein, must necessarily cease, and so every one return to the state he was in before, with a liberty to shift for himself, and provide for his own safety, as he thinks fit, in some other society. Whenever the *society is dissolved*, it is certain the government of that society cannot remain. Thus conquerors swords often cut up governments by the roots, and mangle societies to pieces, separating the subdued or scattered multitude from the protection of, and dependence on, that society which ought to have preserved them from violence. The world is too well instructed in, and too forward to allow of, this way of dissolving of governments, to need any more to be said of it; and there wants not much argument to prove, that where the *society is dissolved*, the government cannot remain; that being as impossible, as for the frame of an house to subsist when the materials of it are scattered and dissipated by a whirl-wind, or jumbled into a confused heap by an earthquake.

§. 212. Besides this over-turning from without, *governments are dissolved from within,*

First, When the *legislative* is *altered.* Civil society being a state of peace, amongst those who are of it, from whom the state of war is excluded by the umpirage, which they have provided in their legislative, for the ending all differences that may arise amongst any of them, it is in their *legislative*, that the members of a common-wealth are united, and combined together into one coherent living body. This *is the soul that gives form, life, and unity*, to the common-wealth: from hence the several members have their mutual influence, sympathy, and connexion: and therefore, when the *legislative* is broken, or *dissolved*, dissolution and death follows: for the *essence and union of the society* consisting in having one will, the legislative, when once established by the majority, has the declaring, and as it were keeping of that will. The *constitution of the legislative* is the first and fundamental act of society, whereby provision is made for the *continuation of their union*, under the direction of persons, and bonds of laws, made by persons authorized thereunto, by the consent and appointment of the people, without which no one man, or number of men, amongst them, can have authority of making laws that shall be binding to the rest. When any one, or more, shall take upon them to make laws, whom the people have not appointed so to do, they make laws without authority, which the people are not therefore bound to obey; by which means they come again to be out of subjection, and may constitute to themselves a *new legislative*, as they think best, being in full liberty to resist the force of those, who without authority would impose any thing upon them. Every one is at the disposure of his own will, when those who had, by the delegation of the society, the declaring of the public will, are excluded from it, and others usurp the place, who have no such authority or delegation.

§. 213. This being usually brought about by such in the common-wealth who misuse the power they have; it is hard to consider it aright, and know at whose door to lay it, without knowing the form of government in which it happens. Let us suppose then the legislative placed in the concurrence of three distinct persons.

1. A single hereditary person, having the constant, supreme, executive power, and with it the power of convoking and dissolving the other two within certain periods of time.

2. An assembly of hereditary nobility.

3. An assembly of representatives chosen, *pro tempore*, by the people. Such a form of government supposed, it is evident,

§. 214. *First*, That when such a single person, or prince, sets up his own arbitrary will in place of the laws, which are the will of the society, declared by the legislative, then the *legislative is changed:* for that being in effect the legislative, whose rules and laws are put in execution, and required to be obeyed; when other laws are set up, and other rules pretended, and inforced, than what the legislative, constituted by the society, have enacted, it is plain that the *legislative is changed.* Whoever introduces new laws, not being thereunto authorized by the fundamental appointment of the society, or subverts the old, disowns and overturns the power by which they were made, and so sets up a *new legislative.*

§. 215. *Secondly,* When the prince hinders the legislative from assembling in its due time, or from acting freely, pursuant to those ends for which it was constituted, the *legislative is altered:* for it is not a certain number of men, no, nor their meeting, unless they have also freedom of debating, and leisure of perfecting, what is for the good of the society, wherein the legislative consists: when these are taken away or altered, so as to deprive the society of the due exercise of their power, the *legislative* is truly altered; for it is not names that constitute governments, but the use and exercise of those powers that were intended to accompany them; so that he, who takes away the freedom, or hinders the acting of the legislative in its due seasons, in effect takes *away the legislative,* and *puts an end to the government.*

§. 216. *Thirdly,* When, by the arbitrary power of the prince, the electors, or ways of election, are altered, without the consent, and contrary to the common interest of the people, there also the *legislative is altered:* for, if others than those whom the society hath authorized thereunto, do chuse, or in another way than what the society hath prescribed, those chosen are not the legislative appointed by the people.

§. 217. *Fourthly,* The delivery also of the people into the subjection of a foreign power, either by the prince, or by the legislative, is certainly a *change of the legislative,* and so a *dissolution of the government:* for the end why people entered into society being to be preserved one intire, free, independent society, to be governed by its own laws; this is lost, whenever they are given up into the power of another.

§. 218. Why, in such a constitution as this, the *dissolution of the government* in these cases is to be imputed to the prince, is evident; because he, having the force, treasure and offices of the state to employ, and often persuading himself, or being flattered by others, that as supreme magistrate he is uncapable of controul; he alone is in a condition to make great advances toward such changes, under pretence of lawful authority, and has it in his hands to terrify or suppress opposers, as factious, seditious, and enemies to the government: whereas no other part of the legislative, or people, is capable by themselves to attempt any alteration of the legislative, without open and visible rebellion, apt enough to be taken notice of, which, when it prevails, produces effects very little different from foreign conquest. Besides, the prince in such a form of government, having the power of dissolving the other parts of the legislative, and thereby rendering them private persons, they can never in opposition to him, or without his concurrence, alter the legislative by a law, his consent being necessary to give any of their decrees that sanction. But yet, so far as the other parts of the legislative any way contribute to any attempt upon the government, and do either promote, or not, what lies in them, hinder such designs, they are guilty, and partake in this, which is certainly the greatest crime men can be guilty of one towards another.

§. 219. There is one way more whereby such a government may be dissolved, and that is, when he who has the supreme executive power, neglects and abandons that charge, so that the laws already made can no longer be put in execution. This is demonstratively to reduce all to anarchy, and so effectually *to dissolve the government:* for laws not being made for themselves, but to be, by their execution, the bonds of the society, to keep every part of the body politic in its due place and function; when that totally ceases, the *government* visibly *ceases,* and the people become a confused multitude, without order or connexion. Where there is no longer the administration of justice, for the securing of men's rights, nor any remaining power within the community to direct the force, or provide for the necessities of the public, there certainly is *no government left.* Where the laws cannot be executed, it is all one as if there were no laws; and a government without laws is, I suppose, a mystery in politics, unconceivable to human capacity, and inconsistent with human society.

§. 220. In these and the like cases, *when the government is dissolved,* the people are at liberty to provide for themselves, by erecting a new legislative, differing from the other, by the change of persons, or form, or both, as they shall find it most for their safety and good: for the *society* can never, by the fault of another, lose the native and original right it has to preserve itself, which can only be done by a settled legislative, and a fair and impartial execution of the laws made by it. But the state of mankind is not so miserable that they are not capable of using this remedy, till it be too late to look for any. To tell *people* they *may provide for themselves,* by erecting a new legislative, when by oppression, artifice, or being delivered over to a foreign power, their old one is gone, is only to tell them, they may expect relief when it is too late, and the evil is past cure. This is in effect no more than to bid them first be slaves, and then to take care of their liberty; and when their chains are on, tell them, they may act like freemen. This, if barely so, is rather mockery than relief; and men can never be secure from tyranny, if there be no means to escape it till they are perfectly under it: and therefore it is, that they have not only a right to get out of it, but to prevent it.

§. 221. There is therefore, secondly, another way whereby *governments are dissolved,* and that is, when the legislative, or the prince, either of them, act contrary to their trust.

First, The *legislative acts against the trust* reposed in them, when they endeavour to invade the property of the subject, and to make themselves, or any part of the community, masters, or arbitrary disposers of the lives, liberties, or fortunes of the people.

§. 222. The reason why men enter into society, is the preservation of their property; and the end why they chuse and authorize a legislative, is, that there may be laws made, and rules set, as guards and fences to the properties of all the members of the society, to limit the power, and moderate the dominion, of every part and member of the society: for since it can never be supposed to be the will of the society, that the legislative should have a power to destroy that which every one designs to secure, by entering into society, and for which the people submitted themselves to legislators of their own making; whenever the *legislators endeavour to take away, and destroy the property of the people,* or to reduce them to slavery under arbitrary power, they put themselves into a state of war with the people, who are thereupon absolved from any farther obedience, and are left to the common refuge, which God hath provided for all men, against force and violence. Whensoever therefore the *legislative* shall transgress this fundamental rule of society; and either by ambition, fear, folly or corruption, *endeavour to grasp* themselves, *or put into the hands of any other, an absolute power* over the lives, liberties, and estates of the people; by this breach of trust they *forfeit the power* the people had put into their hands for quite contrary ends, and it devolves to the people, who have a right to resume their original liberty, and, by the establishment of a new legislative, (such as they shall think fit) provide for their own safety and security, which is the end for which they are in society. What I have said here, concerning the legislative in general, holds true also concerning the supreme executor, who having a double trust put in him, both to have a part in the legislative, and the supreme execution of the law, acts against both, when he goes about to set up his own arbitrary will as the law of the society. He *acts* also *contrary to his trust*, when he either employs the force, treasure, and offices of the society, to corrupt the *representatives*, and gain them to his purposes; or openly pre-engages the *electors*, and prescribes to their choice, such, whom he has, by sollicitations, threats, promises, or otherwise, won to his designs; and employs them to bring in such, who have promised before-hand what to vote, and what to enact. Thus to regulate candidates and electors, and new-model the ways of election, what is it but to cut up the government by the roots, and poison the very fountain of public security? for the people having reserved to themselves the choice of their *representatives*, as the fence to their properties, could do it for no other end, but that they might always be freely chosen, and so chosen, freely act, and advise, as the necessity of the common-wealth, and the public good should, upon examination, and mature debate, be judged to require. This, those who give their votes before they hear the debate, and have weighed the reasons on all sides, are not capable of doing. To prepare such an assembly as this, and endeavour to set up the declared abettors of his own will, for the true *representatives* of the people, and the law-makers of the society, is certainly as great a *breach of trust*, and as perfect a declaration of a design to subvert the government, as is possible to be met with. To which, if one shall add rewards and punishments visibly employed to the same end, and all the arts of perverted law made use of, to take off and destroy all that stand in the way of such a design, and will not comply and consent to betray the liberties of their country, it will be past doubt what is doing. What power they ought to have in the society, who thus employ it contrary to the trust went along with it in its first institution, is easy to determine; and one cannot but see, that he, who has once attempted any such thing as this, cannot any longer be trusted.

§. 223. To this perhaps it will be said, that the people being ignorant, and always discontented, to lay the foundation of government in the unsteady opinion and uncertain humour of the people, is to expose it to certain ruin; and *no government will be able long to subsist*, if the people may set up a new legislative, whenever they take offence at the old one. To this I answer, Quite the contrary. People are not so easily got out of their old forms, as some are apt to suggest. They are hardly to be prevailed with to amend the acknowledged faults in the frame they have been accustomed to. And if there be any original defects, or adventitious ones introduced by time, or corruption; it is not an easy thing to get them changed, even when all the world sees there is an opportunity for it. This slowness and aversion in the people to quit their old constitutions, has, in the many revolutions which have been seen in this kingdom, in this and former ages, still kept us to, or, after some interval of fruitless attempts, still brought us back again to our old legislative of king, lords and commons: and whatever provocations have made the crown be taken from some of our princes heads, they never carried the people so far as to place it in another line.

§. 224. But it will be said, this *hypothesis* lays a *ferment for* frequent *rebellion*. To which I answer,

First, No more than any other *hypothesis:* for when the people are made miserable, and find themselves *exposed to the ill usage of arbitrary power*, cry up their governors, as much as you will, for sons of *Jupiter*; let them be sacred and divine, descended, or authorized from heaven; give them out for whom or what you please, the same will happen. *The people generally ill treated*, and contrary to right, will be ready upon any occasion to ease themselves of a burden that sits heavy upon them. They will wish, and seek for the opportunity, which in the change, weakness and accidents of human affairs, seldom delays long to offer itself. He must have lived but a little while in the world, who has not seen examples of this in his time; and he must have read very little, who cannot produce examples of it in all sorts of governments in the world.

§. 225. *Secondly*, I answer, such *revolutions happen* not upon every little mismanagement in public affairs. *Great mistakes* in the ruling part, many wrong and inconvenient laws, and all the *slips* of human frailty, will be *born by the people* without mutiny or murmur. But if a long train of abuses, prevarications and artifices, all tending the same way, make the design visible to the people, and they cannot but feel what they lie under, and see whither they are going; it is not to be wondered, that they should then rouze themselves, and endeavour to put the rule into such hands which may secure to them the ends for which government was at first erected; and without which, ancient names, and specious forms, are so far from being better, that they are much worse, than the state of nature, or pure anarchy; the inconveniencies being all as great and as near, but the remedy farther off and more difficult.

§. 226. *Thirdly*, I answer, that *this doctrine* of a power in the people of providing for their safety a-new, by a new legislative, when their legislators have acted contrary to their trust, by invading their property, is *the best fence against rebellion*, and the probablest means to hinder it: for *rebellion* being an opposition, not to persons, but authority, which is founded only in the constitutions and laws of the government; those, whoever they be, who by force break through, and by force justify their violation of them, are truly and properly *rebels:* for when men, by entering into society and civil-government, have excluded force, and introduced laws for the preservation of property, peace, and unity amongst themselves, those who set up force again in opposition to the laws, do *rebellare*, that is, bring back again the state of war, and are properly rebels: which they who are in power, (by the pretence they have to authority, the temptation of force they have in their hands, and the flattery of those about them) being likeliest to do; the properest way to prevent the evil, is to shew them the danger and injustice of it, who are under the greatest temptation to run into it.

§. 227. In both the fore-mentioned cases, when either the legislative is changed, or the legislators act contrary to the end for which they were constituted; those who are guilty are *guilty of rebellion:* for if any one by force takes away the established legislative of any society, and the laws by them made, pursuant to their trust, he thereby takes away the umpirage, which every one had consented to, for a peaceable decision of all their controversies, and a bar to the state of war amongst them. They, who remove, or change the legislative, take away this decisive power, which no body can have, but by the appointment and consent of the people; and so destroying the authority which the people did, and no body else can set up, and introducing a power which the people hath not authorized, they actually *introduce a state of war*, which is that of force without authority: and thus, by removing the legislative established by the society, (in whose decisions the people acquiesced and united, as to that of their own will) they untie the knot, and *expose the people a-new to the state of war*. And if those, who by force take away the legislative, are *rebels*, the *legislators* themselves, as has been shewn, can be no less esteemed so; when they, who were set up for the protection, and preservation of the people, their liberties and properties, shall by force invade and endeavour to take them away; and so they putting themselves into a state of war with those who made them the protectors and guardians of their peace, are properly, and with the greatest aggravation, *rebellantes*, rebels.

§. 228. But if they, who say *it lays a foundation for rebellion*, mean that it may occasion civil wars, or intestine broils, to tell the people they are absolved from obedience when illegal attempts are made upon their liberties or properties, and may oppose the unlawful violence of those who were their magistrates, when they invade their properties contrary to the trust put in them; and that therefore this doctrine is not to be allowed, being so destructive to the peace of the world: they may as well say, upon the same ground, that honest men may not oppose robbers or pirates, because this may occasion disorder or bloodshed. If any *mischief* come in such cases, it is not to be charged upon him who defends his own right, but *on him that invades* his neighbours. If the innocent honest man must quietly quit all he has, for peace sake, to him who will lay violent hands upon it, I desire it may be considered, what a kind of peace there will be in the world, which consists only in violence and rapine; and which is to be maintained only for the benefit of robbers and oppressors. Who would not think it an admirable peace betwix the mighty and the mean, when the lamb, without resistance, yielded his throat to be torn by the imperious wolf? *Polyphemus's* den gives us a perfect pattern of such a peace, and such a government, wherein *Ulysses* and his companions had nothing to do, but quietly to suffer themselves to be devoured. And no doubt *Ulysses*, who was a prudent man, preached up *passive obedience*, and exhorted them to a quiet submission, by representing to them of what concernment peace was to mankind; and by shewing the inconveniences might happen, if they should offer to resist *Polyphemus*, who had now the power over them.

§. 229. The end of government is the good of mankind; and which is *best for mankind*, that the people should be always exposed to the boundless will of tyranny, or that the rulers should be sometimes liable to be opposed, when they grow exorbitant in the use of their power, and employ it for the destruction, and not the preservation of the properties of their people?

§. 230. Nor let any one say, that mischief can arise from hence, as often as it shall please a busy head, or turbulent spirit, to desire the alteration of the government. It is true, such men may stir, whenever they please; but it will be only to their own just ruin and perdition: for till the mischief be grown general, and the ill designs of the rulers become visible, or their attempts sensible to the greater part, the people, who are more disposed to suffer than right themselves by resistance, are not apt to stir. The examples of particular injustice, or oppression of here and there an unfortunate man, moves them not. But if they universally have a persuasion, grounded upon manifest evidence, that designs are carrying on against their liberties, and the general course and tendency of things cannot but give them strong suspicions of the evil intention of their governors, who is to be blamed for it? Who can help it, if they, who might avoid it, bring themselves into this suspicion? Are the people to be blamed, if they have the sense of rational creatures, and can think of things no otherwise than as they find and feel them? And is it not rather *their fault*, who put things into such a posture, that they would not have them thought to be as they are? I grant, that the pride, ambition, and turbulency of private men have sometimes caused great disorders in common-wealths, and factions have been fatal to states and kingdoms. But whether *the mischief* hath *oftener* begun *in the peoples wantonness*, and a desire to cast off the lawful authority of their rulers, or *in the rulers insolence*, and endeavours to get and exercise an arbitrary power over their people; whether oppression, or disobedience, gave the first rise to the disorder, I leave it to impartial history to determine. This I am sure, whoever, either ruler or subject, by force goes about to invade the rights of either prince or people, and lays the foundation for *overturning* the constitution and frame of *any just government*, is highly guilty of the greatest crime, I think, a man is capable of, being to answer for all those mischiefs of blood, rapine, and desolation, which the breaking to pieces of governments bring on a country. And he who does it, is justly to be esteemed the common enemy and pest of mankind, and is to be treated accordingly.

§. 231. That *subjects* or *foreigners*, attempting by force on the properties of any people, may be *resisted* with force, is agreed on all hands. But that *magistrates*, doing the same thing, may be *resisted*, hath of late been denied: as if those who had the greatest privileges and advantages by the law, had thereby a power to break those laws, by which alone they were set in a better place than their brethren: whereas their offence is thereby the greater, both as being ungrateful for the greater share they have by the law, and breaking also that trust, which is put into their hands by their brethren.

§. 232. Whosoever uses *force without right*, as every one does in society, who does it without law, puts himself into a *state of war*

with those against whom he so uses it; and in that state all former
ties are cancelled, all other rights cease, and every one has a right to
defend himself, and *to resist the aggressor.* This is so evident, that
Barclay himself, that great assertor of the power and sacredness of
kings, is forced to confess, That it is lawful for the people, in some
cases, to *resist* their king; and that too in a chapter, wherein he
pretends to shew, that the divine law shuts up the people from all
manner of rebellion. Whereby it is evident, even by his own doctrine, that, since they may in some cases *resist*, all resisting of
princes is not rebellion. His words are these. *Quod siquis dicat,*
Ergone populus tyrannicae crudelitati & furori jugulum semper
praebebit? Ergone multitudo civitates suas fame, ferro, & flammâ
vastari, seque, conjuges, & liberos fortunae ludibrio & tyranni
libidini exponi, inque omnia vitae pericula omnesque miserias &
molestias a rege deduci patientur? Num illis quod omni animantium
generi est á naturâ tributum, denegari debet, ut sc. vim vi repellant,
seseq; ab injuriâ tueantur? Huic breviter responsum sit, Populo
universo negari defensionem, quae juris naturalis est, neque ul-
tionem quae praeter naturam est adversus regem concedi debere.
Quapropter si rex non in singulares tantum personas aliquot
privatum odium exerceat, sed corpus etiam reipublicae, cujus ipse
caput est, i. e. totum populum, vel insignem aliquam ejus partem
immani & intolerandâ saevitiâ seu tyrannide divexet; populo,
quidem hoc casu resistendi ac tuendi se ab injuriâ potestas competit,
sed tuendi se tantum, non enim in principem invadendi: & restituen-
dae injuriae illatae, non recedendi à debitâ reverentiâ propter accep-
tam injuriam. Praesentem denique impetum propulsandi non vim
praeteritam ulciscenti jus habet. Horum enim alterum à naturâ est,
ut vitam scilicet corpusque tueamur. Alterum vero contra naturam,
ut inferior de superiori supplicium sumat. Quod itaque populus
malum, antequam factum sit, impedire potest, ne fiat, id postquam
factum est, in regem authorem sceleris vindicare non potest:
populus igitur hoc ampliùs quam privatus quispiam habet: quod
huic, vel ipsis adversariis judicibus, excepto Buchanano, nullum nisi
in patientia remedium superest. Cùm ille si intolerabilis tyrannus est
(modicum enim ferre omnino debet) resistere cum reverentiâ possit,
Barclay contra Monarchom. l. iii. c. 8.

In *English* thus.

§. 233. *But if any one should ask, Must the people then always*

*lay themselves open to the cruelty and rage of tyranny? Must they
see their cities pillaged, and laid in ashes, their wives and children
exposed to the tyrant's lust and fury, and themselves and families
reduced by their king to ruin, and all the miseries of want and oppression, and yet sit still? Must men alone be debarred the common
privilege of opposing force with force, which nature allows so freely
to all other creatures for their preservation from injury? I answer:
Self-defence is a part of the law of nature; nor can it be denied the
community, even against the king himself: but to revenge
themselves upon him, must by no means be allowed them; it being
not agreeable to that law. Wherefore if the king shall shew an
hatred, not only to some particular persons, but sets himself against
the body of the common-wealth, whereof he is the head, and shall,
with intolerable ill usage, cruelly tyrannize over the whole, or a
considerable part of the people, in this case the people have a right
to resist and defend themselves from injury: but it must be with this
caution, that they only defend themselves, but do not attack their
prince: they may repair the damages received, but must not for any
provocation exceed the bounds of due reverence and respect. They
may repulse the present attempt, but must not revenge past
violences: for it is natural for us to defend life and limb, but that an
inferior should punish a superior, is against nature. The mischief
which is designed them, the people may prevent before it be done;
but when it is done, they must not revenge it on the king, though
author of the villany. This therefore is the privilege of the people in
general, above what any private person hath; that particular men
are allowed by our adversaries themselves (Buchanan only ex-
cepted) to have no other remedy but patience; but the body of the
people may with respect resist intolerable tyranny; for when it is
but moderate, they ought to endure it.*

§. 234. Thus far that great advocate of monarchical power
allows of *resistance.*

§. 235. It is true, he has annexed two limitations to it, to no purpose:

First, He says, it must be with reverence.

Secondly, It must be without retribution, or punishment; and the
reason he gives is, *because an inferior cannot punish a superior.*

First, How to *resist force without striking again,* or how to *strike
with reverence,* will need some skill to make intelligible. He that
shall oppose an assault only with a shield to receive the blows, or in
any more respectful posture, without a sword in his hand, to abate

the confidence and force of the assailant, will quickly be at an end of his *resistance,* and will find such a defence serve only to draw on himself the worse usage. This is as ridiculous a way of *resisting,* as *Juvenal* thought it of fighting; *ubi tu pulsas, ego vapulo tantum.* And the success of the combat will be unavoidably the same he there describes it:

> —— *Libertas pauperis haec est:*
> *Pulsatus rogat, & pugnis concisus, adorat,*
> *Ut liceat paucis cum dentibus inde reverti.*

This will always be the event of such an imaginary *resistance,* where men may not strike again. He therefore *who may resist, must be allowed to strike.* And then let our author, or any body else, join a knock on the head, or a cut on the face, with as much *reverence* and *respect* as he thinks fit. He that can reconcile blows and reverence, may, for aught I know, desire for his pains, a civil, respectful cudgeling where-ever he can meet with it.

Secondly, As to his second, *An inferior cannot punish a superior;* that is true, generally speaking, whilst he is his superior. But to resist force with force, being *the state of war* that *levels the parties,* cancels all former relation of reverence, respect, and *superiority:* and then the odds that remains, is, that he, who opposes the unjust agressor, has this *superiority* over him, that he has a right, when he prevails, to punish the offender, both for the breach of the peace, and all the evils that followed upon it. *Barclay* therefore, in another place, more coherently to himself, denies it to be lawful to *resist* a king in any case. But he there assigns two cases, whereby a king may un-king himself. His words are,

Quid ergo, nulline casus incidere possunt quibus populo sese erigere atque in regem impotentius dominantem arma capere & invadere jure suo suâque authoritate liceat? Nulli certe quamdiu rex manet. Semper enim ex divinis id obstat, Regem honorificato; & qui potestati resistit, Dei ordinationi resisit: *non aliàs igitur in eum populo potestas est quam si id committat propter quod ipso jure rex esse desinat. Tunc enim se ipse principatu exuit atque in privatis constituit liber: hoc modo populus & superior efficitur, reverso ad eum sc. jure illo quod ante regem inauguratum in interregno habuit. At sunt paucorum generum commissa ejusmodi quae hunc effectum pariunt. At ego cum plurima animo perlustrem, duo tantum invenio, duos, inquam, casus quibus rex ipso facto ex rege non regem*

*se facit & omni honore & dignitate regali atque in subditos potestate
destituit; quorum etiam meminit* Winzerus. *Horum unus est, Si
regnum disperdat, quemadmodum de Nerone fertur, quod is nempe
senatum populumque Romanum, atque adeo urbem ipsam ferro
flammaque vastare, ac novas sibi sedes quaerere decrevisset. Et de
Caligula, quod palam denunciarit se neque civem neque principem
senatui amplius fore, inque animo habuerit interempto utriusque
ordinis electissimo quoque* Alexandriam *commigrare, ac ut
populum uno ictu interimeret, unam ei cervicem optavit. Talia cum
rex aliquis meditatur & molitur serio, omnem regnandi curam &
animum ilico abjicit, ac proinde imperium in subditos amittit, ut
dominus servi pro derelicto habiti dominium.*

  §. 236. *Alter casus est, Si rex in alicujus clientelam se contulit, ac
regnum quod liberum à majoribus & populo traditum accepit,
alienae ditioni mancipavit. Nam tunc quamvis forte non ea mente id
agit populo plane ut incommodet: tamen quia quod praecipuum est
regiae dignitatis amifit, ut summus scilicet in regno secundum Deum
sit, & solo Deo inferior, atque populum etiam totum ignorantem vel
invitum, cujus libertatem sartam & tectam conservare debuit, in
alterius gentis ditionem & potestatem dedidit; hac velut quadam
regni ab alienatione effecit, ut nec quod ipse in regno imperium
habuit retineat, nec in eum cui collatum voluit, juris quicquam
transferat; atque ita eo facto liberum jam & suae potestatis populum
relinquit, cujus rei exemplum unum annales Scotici suppeditant.*
Barclay contra Monarchom. 1. iii. c. 16.

Which in English runs thus.

  §. 237. *What then, can there no case happen wherein the people
may of right, and by their own authority, help themselves, take
arms, and set upon their king, imperiously domineering over them?
None at all, whilst he remains a king.* Honour the king, *and* he that
resists the power, resists the ordinance of God; *are divine oracles
that will never permit it. The people therefore can never come by a
power over him, unless he does something that makes him cease to
be a king: for then he divests himself of his crown and dignity, and
returns to the state of a private man, and the people become free
and superior, the power which they had in the* interregnum, *before
they crowned him king, devolving to them again. But there are but
few miscarriages which bring the matter to this state. After considering it well on all sides, I can find but two. Two cases there are, I
say, whereby a king,* ipso facto, *becomes no king, and loses all*

power and regal authority over his people; which are also taken notice of by Winzerus.

The first is, If he endeavour to overturn the government, that is, if he have a purpose and design to ruin the kingdom and common-wealth, as it is recorded of Nero, *that he resolved to cut off the senate and people of* Rome, *lay the city waste with fire and sword, and then remove to some other place. And of* Caligula, *that he openly declared, that he would be no longer a head to the people or senate, and that he had it in his thoughts to cut off the worthiest men of both ranks, and then retire to* Alexandria: *and he wisht that the people had but one neck, that he might dispatch them all at a blow. Such designs as these, when any king harbours in his thoughts, and seriously promotes, he immediately gives up all care and thought of the common-wealth; and consequently forfeits the power of governing his subjects, as a master does the dominion over his slaves whom he hath abandoned.*

§. 238. *The other case is, When a king makes himself the depen-dent of another, and subjects his kingdom which his ancestors left him, and the people put free into his hands, to the dominion of another: for however perhaps it may not be his intention to pre-judice the people; yet because he has hereby lost the principal part of regal dignity,* viz. *to be next and immediately under God, supreme in his kingdom; and also because he betrayed or forced his people, whose liberty he ought to have carefully preserved, into the power and dominion of a foreign nation. By this, as it were, aliena-tion of his kingdom, he himself loses the power he had in it before, without transferring any the least right to those on whom he would have bestowed it; and so by this act sets the people free, and leaves them at their own disposal. One example of this is to be found in the* Scotch *Annals.*

§. 239. In these cases Barclay, the great champion of absolute monarchy, is forced to allow, that a king may be *resisted,* and *ceases to be a king.* That is, in short, not to multiply cases, in what-soever he has *no authority,* there he is *no king,* and may be *resisted:* for wheresoever the *authority ceases, the king ceases too,* and becomes like other men who have no authority. And these two cases he instances in, differ little from those above mentioned, to be destructive to governments, only that he has omitted the principle from which his doctrine flows: and that is, the breach of trust, in not preserving the form of government agreed on, and in not in-tending the end of government itself, which is the public good and preservation of property. When a king has dethroned himself, and

put himself in a state of war with his people, what shall hinder them
from prosecuting him who is no king, as they would any other man,
who has put himself into a state of war with them, *Barclay*, and
those of his opinion, would do well to tell us. This farther I desire
may be taken notice of out of *Barclay*, that he says, *The mischief
that is designed them, the people may prevent before it be done:*
whereby he allows *resistance* when tyranny is but in design. *Such
designs as these* (says he) *when any king harbours in his thoughts
and seriously promotes, he immediately gives up all care and
thought of the common-wealth;* so that, according to him, the
neglect of the public good is to be taken as an evidence of such
design, or at least for a sufficient cause of *resistance*. And the reason
of all, he gives in these words, *Because he betrayed or forced his
people, whose liberty he ought carefully to have preserved.* What
he adds, *into the power and dominion of a foreign nation*, signifies
nothing, the fault and forfeiture lying in the loss of their *liberty*,
which he *ought to have preserved*, and not in any distinction of the
persons to whose dominion they were subjected. The peoples right
is equally invaded, and their liberty lost, whether they are made
slaves to any of their own, or a *foreign nation;* and in this lies the injury, and against this only have they the right of defence. And there
are instances to be found in all countries, which shew, that it is not
the change of nations in the persons of their governors, but the
change of government, that gives the offence. *Bilson*, a bishop of
our church, and a great stickler for the power and prerogative of
princes, does, if I mistake not, in his treatise of *Christian subjection*,
acknowledge, that *princes may forfeit their power*, and their title to
the obedience of their subjects; and if there needed authority in a
case where reason is so plain, I could send my reader to *Bracton*,
Fortescue, and the author of *the Mirrour*, and others, writers that
cannot be suspected to be ignorant of our government, or enemies
to it. But I thought *Hooker* alone might be enough to satisfy those
men, who relying on him for their ecclesiastical polity, are by a
strange fate carried to deny those principles upon which he builds it.
Whether they are herein made the tools of cunninger workmen, to
pull down their own fabric, they were best look. This I am sure,
their civil policy is so new, so dangerous, and so destructive to both
rulers and people, that as former ages never could bear the
broaching of it; so it may be hoped, those to come, redeemed from
the impositions of these *Egyptian* under-task-masters, will abhor
the memory of such servile flatterers, who, whilst it seemed to serve
their turn, resolved all government into absolute tyranny, and

would have all men born to, what their mean souls fitted them for, slavery.

§. 240. Here. It is like, the common question will be made, *Who shall be judge*, whether the prince or legislative act contrary to their trust? This, perhaps, ill-affected and factious men may spread amongst the people, when the prince only makes use of his due prerogative. To this I reply, *The people shall be judge;* for who shall be *judge* whether his trustee or deputy acts well, and according to the trust reposed in him, but he who deputes him, and must, by having deputed him, have still a power to discard him, when he fails in his trust? If this be reasonable in particular cases of private men, why should it be otherwise in that of the greatest moment, where the welfare of millions is concerned, and also where the evil, if not prevented, is greater, and the redress very difficult, dear, and dangerous?

§. 241. But farther, this question, *(Who shall be judge?)* cannot mean, that there is no judge at all: for where there is no judicature on earth, to decide controversies amongst men, *God* in heaven is *judge*. He alone, it is true, is judge of the right. But *every man* is *judge* for himself, as in all other cases, so in this, whether another hath put himself into a state of war with him, and whether he should appeal to the Supreme Judge, as *Jeptha* did.

§. 242. If a controversy arise betwixt a prince and some of the people, in a matter where the law is silent, or doubtful, and the thing be of great consequence, I should think the proper *umpire,* in such a case, should be the body of the *people:* for in cases where the prince hath a trust reposed in him, and is dispensed from the common ordinary rules of the law; there, if any men find themselves aggrieved, and think the prince acts contrary to, or beyond that trust, who so proper to *judge* as the body of the *people,* (who, at first, lodged that trust in him) how far they meant it should extend? But if the prince, or whoever they be in the administration, decline that way of determination, the appeal then lies no where but to heaven; force between either persons, who have no known superior on earth, or which permits no appeal to a judge on earth, being properly a state of war, wherein the appeal lies only to heaven; and in that state the *injured party must judge* for himself, when he will think fit to make use of that appeal, and put himself upon it.

§. 243. To conclude, The *power that every individual gave the society,* when he entered into it, can never revert to the individuals again, as long as the society lasts, but will always remain in the community; because without this there can be no community, no common-wealth, which is contrary to the original agreement: so also when the society hath placed the legislative in any assembly of men, to continue in them and their successors, with direction and authority for providing such successors, *the legislative can never revert to the people* whilst that government lasts; because having provided a legislative with power to continue for ever, they have given up their political power to the legislative, and cannot resume it. But if they have set limits to the duration of their legislative, and made this supreme power in any person, or assembly, only temporary; or else, when by the miscarriages of those in authority, it is forfeited; upon the forfeiture, or at the determination of the time set, *it reverts to the society*, and the people have a right to act as supreme, and continue the legislative in themselves; or erect a new form, or under the old form place it in new hands, as they think good.

FINIS.

C. B. MACPHERSON was born in Toronto, Canada in 1911. From 1935 to his death in 1987, he taught primarily at the University of Toronto, as Lecturer in Political Economy, as Professor of Political Science, and finally, as University Professor. In 1979 he received the Benjamin E. Lippincott Award of the American Political Science Association for his *Political Theory of Possessive Individualism: Hobbes to Locke*. He is author also of *Democracy in Alberta: the Theory and Practice of a Quasi-Party System; The Real World of Democracy; Democratic Theory: Essays in Retrieval;* and *The Life and Times of Liberal Democracy.*

A festschrift honoring Professor Macpherson, edited by Alkis Kontos, entitled *Powers, Possessions and Freedom: Essays in Honor of C. B. Macpherson*, was published in 1979.